Antietam Shadows

Also by the Author

September Suspense: Lincoln's Union in Peril

Antietam Revealed

Harpers Ferry Under Fire: A Border Town during the Civil War

History & Tour Guide to Stonewall Jackson's Battle of Harpers Ferry

Available at www.harpersferryhistory.org. Sales proceeds help benefit the Harpers Ferry Park Association, a nonprofit that supports Harpers Ferry National Historical Park.

Antietam Shadows

Mystery, Myth & Machination

Dennis E. Frye

Antietam Rest Publishing

Sharpsburg, Maryland

Antietam Shadows: Mystery, Myth & Machination © 2018 Dennis E. Frye

Printed in the United States of America by
Antietam Rest Publishing

Maps & cover designed by Silverback Designs
Cover photo by Kathy Tustanowski
Produced by High Peaks Publishing

To order,
Harpers Ferry Park Association
P.O. Box 197
Harpers Ferry, WV 25425
304.535.6881
www.harpersferryhistory.org

ISBN 978-0-9854119-2-3

[I]t is the province of the historian to find out, not what was, but what is.

—Henry David Thoreau

Table of Contents

CHAPTER 1
Beware History

What is history but a fable agreed upon.
—Napoleon Bonaparte[1]

NAPOLEON'S ADMONITION sent me reeling.

Was he suggesting history is the original "fake news"?

My initial response was indignation. I glared at Dr. James Holland from my seat in the middle of the front row. Day One of my junior year at Shepherd College had commenced. Enthused about returning to the classroom, I felt deflated when Professor Holland launched this missile of Napoleonic doubt, as he opened his modern European history course. I sensed my exhilaration for history, never before in doubt, experiencing existential evaporation.

Since grade school, I had charted my course toward a career as a professional historian. History, I felt certain, was my destiny. I enjoyed exploring history. I enjoyed presenting history, researching history, writing history and performing history. I grew up surrounded by history, and I played on grounds where history had occurred. History consumed me.

Suddenly, though, my bespectacled, gray-haired distinguished and respected professor with the baritone voice informed me history was, well . . . a fraud.

Sacrilege!

How can we deny history? It precedes us, informs us, guides us. Literally, through genetics, it inhabits us. History, like it or not, dictates who we are, what we are and why we are. History is not past, but present—existing with every breath. Ralph Waldo Emerson mused in his transcendental essay on history: "There is a relation between the hours of our life and the centuries of time."[2] We know too that history is not old and stale, but vibrant and omnipresent—we create new history every day.

But the question that startled me forty years ago still pounds in my soul today—is history real?

I've had four decades to ruminate on this reality question, and I've developed some conclusions.

History is represented as facts.

It is not.

History is deemed immutable.

Not so.

History is declared as truth.

Nein. Nyet. Non.

These are strange pontifications coming from the pen of a professional historian. But I am not alone. Philosopher Emerson himself cast doubt upon the veracity of history: "Time dissipates to shining ether the solid angularity of facts. No anchor, no cable, no fences, avail to keep fact a fact."[3]

So what, then, is history?

Opinion.

"All history becomes subjective," postulates Emerson. "[I]n other words, there is properly no history."[4]

Beware opinion. This principle is fundamental to the contents of this volume. History, as a record of human activity, is flawed because humans insert their opinions into the record, upon the onset of the recording.

Our partiality infraction is no sin, but natural. Humans perceive reality; we do not record reality.

History, at its foundation, is an act of human observation. But as thinking beings, we immediately lend prejudice to what we witness. Our brains transform an observation into a thought, and at that moment, reality ceases. Perception becomes the product of the thought. Consider for a moment the confusion of jurors when the same witnesses see the same thing at the same time, but the recollection of each is different. Like a witness, history also suffers from the flaws of individual imperfection.

Beware perception. Perception, by itself, is not the only detractor from history's reality. Prejudice influences the story as well. And prejudice is an expression of point of view. We apply point of view to everything. It's inescapable. It explains how we watch the same debate and hear the same words, but depart without the same conclusions.

Beware point of view. Be on the lookout for it. Once you discern it, you'll discover that history, first and foremost, should exist for debate—not for foregone conclusions. Just because the historian writes it doesn't mean that it's sacred. Historians are influenced by their own cultures and defined by their own prejudices. No neutral historian exists, nor has one ever existed. Your job, as a discerning observer, is to uncover the historian's agenda to determine the historian's approach, and then inject your own thinking into the argument. Then you have history at its best—as debate.

Since this book uses the Civil War as a means to examine history, let's offer an example from that tumultuous era that illustrates point of view.

The place: Charleston Harbor, South Carolina. The event: Americans attacking Americans. The Civil War erupts as Palmetto State Confederates bombard the U.S. garrison at Fort Sumter. The Stars and Stripes are dropped down in surrender. The point of view: Southern historians looked upon it as an act of independence; Northern historians termed it treason. So which is it?

Another example of point of view is drawn from the outset of the Civil War. Abolitionist John Brown (from New England) was executed for his failed attack on the U.S. Arsenal at Harpers Ferry (which was still in Virginia then, and the largest slave-holding state). Northern historians hailed Brown as a martyr and freedom fighter. Southern histories condemned him as a terrorist and the devil incarnate. So who is right? Who is wrong?

Beware the judge. Here we discover a significant trap in history—the tendency to judge. Are people only right? Or only wrong? Is there nothing in between? St. Matthew (7:2), in the English of

King James, quotes Jesus as saying: "For with what judgment ye judge, ye shall be judged." But historians have little respect for this edict and practice judgment often. We like to condemn and we like to extol. We especially enjoy applying our own standards to those living in the past, and then judging the past for failing to abide by our modern standards.

This reminds me of our efforts to purge from our history American statesmen who were slaveholders. Slavery is abhorrent to us today. Most (it should be all) Americans are embarrassed that the "land of the free" was once the "land of the slave." But in the time of George Washington and Thomas Jefferson, slavery was the law of the land, legal and accepted, and justified by its defenders who cited slavery's existence throughout the Bible. Should we strip away the name of a high school because these men owned slaves? Or should we utilize history classes in those schools to discuss the discrepancies between "all men are created equal" and the contradiction of slavery?

Beware simplistic history. In our world of the twenty-second sound bite and the thirty-second ad, we shun complexity. We want it straight, fast, easy and uncomplicated. If we can't scroll it and grab it, we don't want to grasp it. But history is meant for thought, not speed. Yet our curricula race through history, offering tons of content, but no time for context. We simplify to beat the school calendar, and the product is a class of history simpletons. Without context, the content has little value and even less meaning. We teach chronology (boring) rather than context (stimulating). And the results are fruitless and futile.

Beware memory. Memory drapes a curtain of opaque fog over the veracity of history. What do I mean? As time fleets, reality flees. The more time passes, the more we forget. What we don't forget, we often exaggerate. Our recollections create a new narrative—a faux history. And when we depend on memory, we tend to layer our own agenda onto the history. This is not necessarily nefarious, but a natural progression that promotes and prolongs one's self interest. This is the folly of any reminiscence.

To my Civil War friends, we in particular are victims of reminiscences. We love a good story, no matter how many years have passed since the end of the Civil War (which ended in 1865, by the way).

So many times have I and others in the trade waxed eloquent with stories told thirty, forty or even fifty years after the war. We label the recollection of the actors "primary" (simply because they were witnesses), and yield to them truth, assuming they are being accurate. What fools we are. Deluded by our penchant to equate reality with reminiscences, we repeat false narratives over and over again. I expose flawed memories in this book. Historians would be well to remember that all memory is flawed.

Beware the historian. Historians wield power. Our research and writings inform the powerful and assist those seeking power. We can abuse our privilege as historians to justify agenda and legitimize power. Or we can use our craft to expose the corrupt and to dethrone convention.

But our most important mission is this—we must investigate history more for its falsehoods than its truths. Historians must challenge the findings of other historians. Trust among historians is an undesirable bond. We should question each other, test each other, debate each other and compete with each other in an infinite search for history's mysteries.

Then, only, will historians earn distinction as the optimum observers and recorders of humanity.

CHAPTER 2
Mentor or Tormentor?

History is the best teacher,
if the teacher merits best.
—The author

HOW MANY OF YOU detest history?

Be honest. It's okay to say you dreaded history classes. Most people do. It's understandable that you rejected history as nothing but rote memorization and ridiculous regurgitation. What's important about a chronological listing of dates? Why do I need to know this? Who cares!

Those of you who are fellow Civil War buffs will smirk and mutter to yourself, I'm not in that crowd. We feel elevated—better than the uninitiated, buttressed by our facts and wisdom that we have accumulated through years of study, and in competition with each other to see who has the most books on our shelves. But we're among the 1 percent (sorry, not in wealth) who can claim knowledge of the Civil War. The rest of our fellow Americans might even have to think for a second when pressed to name which president came first—Lincoln or Washington. Or perhaps they grapple with more remote questions, such as why were the combatants' colors blue and gray rather than red and blue?

History is in a sorry state in our country. That's really no surprise. It's our fault. We do our best to make history innocuous, insidious and irrelevant. If it teaches us nothing practical, why teach it?

Remember the stereotypical image of the football coach as the history teacher? You know, the idea that only a jock could teach something as dumb as history? I knew football coaches who taught history and produced undefeated seasons. Perhaps they were so successful because they studied successes and failures throughout history, and applied those lessons to the gridiron. Perhaps they learned motivation by studying Churchill; teamwork through analyzing Eisenhower; and fortitude by emulating Lincoln. Perhaps they really were the best teachers of history.

In our current world of STEM (Science, Technology, Engineering, Math), we have no room, no time, and no patience for the study of people responding to dilemmas (history); selecting options (history); making choices (history); and living with the consequences—forever (history).

Each of us creates history every day. It's so elementary, and so pervasive, we don't think of it as history. But let's pause, and think for a moment about how we generate our own history. Do you not face dilemmas each day? Aren't various options available for you to resolve your issues? Do you not make a choice after careful consideration? And ultimately, aren't you either the victor or victim as you're chained to the consequences of your choice? This is the human process of history. You're part of history. The very fact that you live means that you are creating history.

So why, then, is history about the past? If it's so current, so immediate, so omnipresent, why is it always presented as something far away and so long, long ago?

That's precisely the problem: it's the presentation of history that kills its meaning and destroys its value.

I know this because kids told me so. While conducting research for a future book I'm writing: "Why Your Kids Hate History (and so did you!)", I interviewed dozens of university students and high school youth who were working as interns or in summer jobs at Harpers Ferry National Historical Park. I asked each this question: Why do kids hate history? The response over and again was this chorus: We don't dislike history, we don't like the way history is taught.

That returns us to history as rote memorization of endless dates and regurgitation of meaningless facts. That is our preferred method of teaching history. In essence, we've distilled history into dates and chronology and removed the humanity. Instead of "his-story" or "her-story", we've removed the character and personality of him and her and condensed these beings into inanimate bits otherwise known as facts.

So sad.

But instead of tormentor, history could be our great mentor. You've heard the hackneyed term, "history repeats itself." Wrong. History doesn't repeat itself—people do. People create history; people produce patterns of behavior; and through study of these patterns, we often are able to predict outcomes. Hence the phrase, "history repeats itself."

Realize it or not, we utilize history as a mentor every day. Though mostly unaware, we learn from history each day we live. Remember when you were a kid and you put your finger into a lit match? History teaches you not to repeat that experiment. On a business scale, every corporation, whether Amazon or the local animal rescue shelter, collects and scrutinizes history every day. They must, or they will cease to exist. Their existence depends upon the examination and analysis (history) of the successes and failures of competitors (history) to avoid their mistakes and better their products. The Army, CIA and FBI employ thousands of historians (they label them "analysts") who compile extensive histories (they call them investigations) of our enemies and criminals as a way to predict behavior and actions. Imagine that—using the past to predict the future. History, you see, is crucial to our safety, well-being and national security—every day.

So, now that we've established that we all create history, that history is essential to our work and jobs, and that history is indispensable to protecting us, perhaps we're open to discarding our distaste for history and replacing it with a discussion about history.

That's the purpose of this volume—for us to discuss history, not memorize it or recite it. We will open our minds for discussion and debate. In other words, assess history as it should be taught.

For my Civil War aficionados who are attuned to history, this book is not about strategy or tactics (I hear the cheers of relief from the rest of you). I do build, however, upon your extensive knowledge of the war. But I will turn upside down so much of what you know. I will challenge you to think differently. I will dispute established historians. I will defy conventional wisdom. I will counter accepted notions with my own forceful contentions—subjects I have been deliberating and debating within myself for more than forty years. I've tested my conclusions before dozens of Civil War audiences, and the responses are what I hoped: "Hmmm . . . I never thought of it that way."

For my friends who are not so steeped in the Civil War, this is a book about human nature—character traits that all of us share—as presented through history. The stories I share are based upon the Civil War—specifically a campaign in the Civil War named Antietam (an-TEE-tum); but you don't need to know anything about the war to relate to the tales herein. You probably never considered that you share character traits with Abraham Lincoln. He was, after all, one of us (human).

My proposition is that history is a great mentor. The best mentors don't provide answers, but ask questions. Here are a few examples we will explore. What will we learn from intentional disobedience? How will we react when our well-conceived plans go haywire? What is the result when we are overconfident? How do we adjust when our schedules are compromised?

History as well teaches us principles of leadership. Should I take this risk? What are the possible outcomes? Do I defy the odds? Is this a moment to be cautious or zealous? If too cautious, what opportunities may pass? If too zealous, what hazards may lurk?

Because humans have been imperfect since the Garden of Eden, we also will witness examples of our worst nature. Bringing harm to others to benefit ourselves is a prime example. Disloyalty, deceit and betrayal are themes. And of course, we have liars, cheaters and thugs (we can't avoid politicians).

This book, in sum, challenges those who love history and encourages those who have run from it.

For those on the run, I hope we can slay the tormentor that's been chasing you.

CHAPTER 3
Let's Agree...We Disagree

Words—so innocent and powerless as they are,
as standing in a dictionary,
how potent for good and evil they become
in the hands of one who knows how to combine them.
—Nathaniel Hawthorne[5]

DISAGREEMENT DEFINES America.

The First Amendment, in effect, ensures our right to disagree. Freedom of religion means we do not have to agree on worship. Freedom of assembly allows us to gather in crowds to demonstrate our disagreements. Freedom of speech permits us to disagree with everybody about everything. Freedom of petition encourages us to disagree with our local, state and federal governments. Freedom of the press ensures disagreement with policy and power and politicians.

America's inception was born in disagreement (brandished at the Boston Tea Party) and its enrichment and evolution were spurred by disagreement (consider the Civil Rights movement). The proposition that the United States is "united" defies our innate propensity for disagreement.

The biggest disagreement in American history resulted in the American Civil War.

We disagreed so much, in fact, that we fought each other for four years, killed each other for four years, and destroyed hundreds of millions of dollars of property on battlefields we created on American soil for four years.

It was our deadliest war. We killed more of us from 1861 to1865 than the human wreckage caused by our enemies in the Revolutionary War, the War of 1812, the Mexican War, the Spanish American War, World War I, World War II, the Korean War and Vietnam War combined.

The title of *Antietam Shadows* is, in fact, taken from the Battle of Antietam—the bloodiest single day in American history. In only twelve hours, 23,000 American soldiers were killed or maimed—not in Western Europe, but in Western Maryland. For perspective, that's four times the casualties we suffered on D-Day and about three times the casualties of 9/11.

So—why?

Why were farmers from Pennsylvania killing farmers from North Carolina? Why were the denizens of New York slaughtering citizens from Savannah? Why were the factory workers of Massachusetts butchering the riverboat operators of Mississippi?

What caused our Civil War?

Still today, citizens of this country cannot agree on what caused the Civil War. Student textbooks in Northern states declare the cause to be slavery. Classes in Southern states establish the supremacy of states' rights as the cause. More than a century and a half after we commenced killing each other over these "causes," we still cannot agree on what caused the killing.

So it's worth a moment to reflect on America's nadir.

Strains over slavery soared into feverish disagreement as the nation wobbled toward its centennial. As the country expanded westward, and new states petitioned to become part of the United States, a struggle for national power ensued between sectional interests.

Reformers in Northern states considered slavery morally corrupt and in violation of the creed set forth in the Declaration of Independence. Southerners countered with justifications for slavery from the Bible. Northern politicians attempted to prohibit slavery's expansion; representatives from the South demanded it. For thirty years, federal elected officials adopted compromise that

Abraham Lincoln. *Courtesy of the Library of Congress.*

maintained a balance of governing power between free states and slave states.

No compromise ended the arguments, however. Instead, tensions were exacerbated and emotions inflamed. Public disagreement over slavery, by the 1850s, had carved a Grand Canyon between the peoples of North and South. Abraham Lincoln, in his unsuccessful run for U.S. Senate in the decade before the Civil War, summarized it best in the quintessential disagreement over slavery in the famous Lincoln/Douglas debates: "A house divided against itself cannot stand. I believe this government cannot endure, permanently half slave and half free. I do not expect the Union to be dissolved—I do not expect the house to fall—but I do expect it will cease to be divided. It will become all one thing, or all the other."[6]

John C. Calhoun, the Southern champion of states' rights, never heard Lincoln's warning. He had gone to his grave, but his declarations echoed through the years: "I never use the word nation in speaking of the United States," pronounced the fiery U.S. Senator from South Carolina, who dominated Southern political intellect for nearly 40 years during the antebellum period. Concerned that the population advantage in the North was subverting Southern interests in the Congress and would ultimately lead to the demise of slavery, Calhoun opined: "I always use the word Union or Confederacy. We are not a nation but a union, a confederacy of equal and sovereign States." [7]

Calhoun persistently preached against the tyranny of the perceived (Northern) majority: "If we do not defend ourselves none will defend us; if we yield we will be more and more pressed as we recede; and if we submit we will be trampled underfoot. I hold concession or compromise to be fatal."

Democracy, without compromise, will fail. Compromise is the solution to unyielding disagreement. Calhoun did not argue for the demise of democracy, but his priority for the federal government trumpeted three S words—Southern, States' rights, and Slavery. "The defense of human liberty against the aggressions of despotic power," Calhoun argued, "have been always the most efficient in States where domestic slavery was to prevail."[8]

What?

Read that again—slowly. Is Calhoun delusional? Or is "despotic power" his term for the federal government? Calhoun believed slave ownership was a fundamental property right, and he feared a centralized and controlling federal government that may seize that right. Though nearly impossible for us to fathom, slave owners considered slaves as property, not as humans. Calhoun was equating property rights with human liberty.

As Calhoun lambasted the legislative power of the Congress, he and his fellow Southerners gained some measure of balance in the executive and judiciary branches. Of the first fifteen presidents, not a single one advocated for slavery's abolition while occupying the White House. Nine of the chief executives hailed from Southern states, and others were Northern Democrats who aligned with the party's Southern base. Supreme Court justices boasting Southern heritage held the majority, and the lower judicial courts, overall, reflected sectional societal interests.

Two upheavals destroyed this delicate balance in the federal system—the Dred Scott decision by the Supreme Court and the election of Abraham Lincoln.

The ultimate arbiter of disagreement in America is the Supreme Court. When Dred Scott, a slave, claimed himself a citizen (a human being), and not a piece of property (the definition of a slave by U.S. and Southern state laws), Scott sued for a determination. In an explosive decision, the Court ruled (7-2) Scott could not claim citizenship, and it postulated further that Congress could not limit the expansion of slavery. It then explained why. Scott represented "beings of an inferior order, and altogether unfit to associate with the white race, either in social or political relations; and so far inferior, that they had no rights which the white man was bound to respect; and that the negro might justly and lawfully be reduced to slavery for his benefit." [9]

The decision ignited a rabid response from Republicans—a nascent political party scarcely three years old. Lincoln, then an Illinois lawyer, stipulated the party's position: "The Republicans inculcate . . . that the negro is a man; that his bondage is cruelly wrong, and that the field of his oppression ought not to be enlarged."

Then Lincoln attacked the opposition party. "The Democrats deny [the slave's] manhood; deny, or dwarf to insignificance, the wrong of his bondage; so far as possible, crush all sympathy for him, and cultivate and excite hatred and disgust against him." [10]

Thus we have the longest and most divisive disagreement in American history—race relations.

When will we agree—to end this disagreement—and eternally agree that "all men are created equal"?

CHAPTER 4
What We Know

You know nothing until you know all;
which is the reason we never know anything.
—Herman Melville[11]

THERE ARE ABSOLUTES in history.

September 11, 2001, is an absolute. Pearl Harbor, the "date which will live in infamy," is December 7, 1941. Neil Armstrong radios from the moon to planet earth, "Houston, Tranquility Base here. The Eagle has landed," on July 20, 1969. The Armistice Day that ended fighting in World War I, "the war to end all wars," was November 11, 1918. Constitution Day, marking the date when the Founders signed the document and submitted it for ratification by the states, is September 17, 1787. Lincoln's Gettysburg Address, some four score and seven years after the Declaration of Independence, is on November 19, 1863.

Note one commonality: dates. Dates are absolutes in history.

The presence of specific people, on a specific date, located at a specific place, and engaged in a specific activity, also can be deemed absolute. As example, Lee surrendered to Grant at the Wilmer McLean house at Appomattox Court House on April 9, 1865.

Beyond such certitudes, nothing is absolute in history.

So, what certainties define the story that is *Antietam Shadows*? What do we know? Here's the scoop:

It's 1862. America had entered its second year of civil war. The United States Army had failed to capture Richmond, Virginia, the capital of the upstart Confederacy. Robert E. Lee, Southern commander of the Army of Northern Virginia, responded with an invasion of the North. Lee's target was Pennsylvania. But first he splashed across the Potomac River, entered the border state of Maryland, and settled at the hamlet of Frederick, only forty miles from Washington. Here Lee stopped and awaited a U.S. response.

Meanwhile, in the Union capital, President Lincoln responded to the invasion emergency and rehired General George McClellan (whom he had recently fired) to lead the defense of the United States. McClellan organized defeated and demoralized U.S. forces, positioned them behind fortifications to protect Washington, and guided the Army of the Potomac into Western Maryland in search of Lee.

As Lee watched for Federal movements, he learned about a problem behind his lines—a U.S. garrison at Harpers Ferry. If ignored, this force potentially could disrupt Lee's rear as he launched into Pennsylvania. So the Rebel commander devised a scheme to eliminate this threat. Lee issued "special orders" on September 9 that divided his army, sending most of it to Harpers Ferry. As this move developed, Lee marched toward the Mason-Dixon Line, stopping at Hagerstown, where he intended to reunite his army after conquering Harpers Ferry.

Then fate intervened. Someone lost a copy of Lee's "special orders," and they fell into enemy hands. Soon after the Union army arrived at Frederick, General McClellan clutched Lee's "lost orders" in his hands. What a discovery!

Flustered at the slow pace of progress at Harpers Ferry (which was behind schedule), and warned about unexpected advances of the Union army, Lee turned away from Pennsylvania and returned to South Mountain. Here battle raged at three mountain gaps on Sunday, September 14. Deeming it impossible to hold the mountain passes on the morrow, Lee ordered his army to retreat back into Virginia, and to halt the still-inconclusive operation at Harpers Ferry. In sum, Lee canceled the invasion.

While headed home to the Old Dominion in the darkness, Lee stopped his tired force near the crossroads village of Sharpsburg and the Antietam Creek. Here he learned that Harpers Ferry finally had capitulated on September 15. Lee abruptly canceled the withdrawal back to the Confederacy, and he ordered the Harpers Ferry detachment to rendezvous promptly with him at Sharpsburg.

As Lee waited, the Union army approached. McClellan knew Harpers Ferry had surrendered, and he knew Lee was strengthening as the Rebels unified. McClellan decided: attack! The Battle of Antietam (coined the Battle of Sharpsburg by the South) commenced at dawn on Wednesday, September 17. It lasted nearly twelve hours. Innocuous sites such as The Cornfield, the West Woods, the Dunker Church, the Sunken Road, the Lower Bridge—all common to locals in their trivial travels—were transformed into iconic national landmarks where American destiny was altered.

Together, these sites played host to the bloodiest single day in American history. More than 23,000 lay dead and wounded, in half a day, before the human slaughter ceased.

Dead Confederate artillerymen in front of the Dunker Church at Antietam. *Courtesy of the Library of Congress.*

The opposing armies were unsettled the next day, but no battle occurred. The next night after the fight, Lee determined withdrawal his best option and the Confederates returned to Virginia. Lee hoped to redeploy and renew the invasion further up the Potomac, but McClellan blocked his river crossing and his attacks momentarily caused a stir at Lee's rear near Shepherdstown.

The invasion ended. Washington was safe. Maryland secured. Pennsylvania's rapid pulse returned to normal. The North acclaimed the campaign as a great victory for the Union. President Lincoln hailed the triumph, sensing it so significant that he issued the Preliminary Emancipation Proclamation on September 22—only five days after Antietam.

Ten months later, Lee attempted a second invasion. It, too, ended in failure, this time at Gettysburg.

End scoop.

■ ■ ■

A SKELETON OF HISTORY is an apt way to describe what you just read—a simple chronology of who, what, where and when. The words are unadorned, and principally present facts. The narrative lacks heart, tugs not at the soul, and purposely avoids hyperbole and emotion. In essence, I removed humanity from history. I didn't tell you a story, full of life and excitement and unknown adventure. Instead, I presented a chalk board of absolutes. Does this remind you of the way you were taught history? The dreaded memorization of dates, followed by the regurgitation of chronology, ensued by erasure from your memory. Does that resurrect school horrors?

I hope that Antietam Shadows is an antonym for the poor presentation of history. History can be fun, exciting, and even entertaining, depending upon its delivery. So here's our mission. Together we will become detectives and investigate mysteries. Together we will challenge convention and uncover myths. Together we will expose Civil War Machiavelli(s) and the art of machination.

Let's enjoy history!

CHAPTER 5
Eight Words

The ability to discriminate between that which is true and that which is false is one of the last attainments of the human mind.
—James Fenimore Cooper[12]

"WE WILL MAKE OUR STAND on those hills."

I have spoken these words, with dramatic flair, countless times when leading guided tours on the Antietam Battlefield.

These are the words of Robert E. Lee.

Lee was worried. The Confederate general unwillingly found himself in a defensive position along the serpentine Antietam Creek in narrow Western Maryland. Lee did not expect this dilemma. He intended to invade Pennsylvania; but the unexpected aggressiveness of his opponent, the Union Army of the Potomac, had foiled that plan. Confounding the situation, Lee knew that his own army was scattered and divided, with two of every three soldiers absent on another assignment, and at least a full day's march distant. Compounding matters, the U.S. forces outnumbered the Rebel chieftain, even had his troops been united.

These problems argued against making a stand. Appearance suggested little could be gained, and much potentially lost. Perhaps a better option was withdrawal, especially since the Virginia border and the Confederate homeland were only three miles away.

Lee, however, appeared adamant: "We will make our stand on those hills." The meaning of the word "stand" signified more im-

21

portance than the standard definition might imply. It was about reputation—the reputation of Lee's army, his country and the general himself.

Lee possessed the brand and bravado of a gamesman. With nerves of steel, he could stare down his opponent, bluff his opponent, dare his opponent and scare his opponent. Lee's unconventional approach to warfare had saved the Confederate capital in Richmond and had sent Union armies reeling and fleeing. For Lee's soldiers, he had become heroic, almost mythical, in victory. Under the guidance of "Marse Robert," as his men affectionately called him, Lee's Rebels believed they could whip any Yankee anywhere at any time.

Lee's chivalric modesty prevented self-adulation, but he showed streaks of stubbornness, and on occasion, rigidity. These ornery human traits surfaced as Lee paced anxiously atop Antietam's rolling hills. Heavy on his mind from the previous day was his first military setback as commander of the Army of Northern Virginia at the Battle of South Mountain. Instead of advancing, he was retreating. Knocked backward, Lee regrouped for round two.

"We will make our stand on those hills."

But did Lee really utter these words?

An apt quotation, indeed it is—powerful, visual, direct and apropos. It defines General Lee.

But what is the source? Historians depend upon sources to write their history. So what is the origin of this quotation?

Since these were General Lee's words, we expect that General Lee recorded them. He did not. No contemporary Lee dispatch used this language. No official Lee report included this phrase. No letter or diary entry by Lee expressed these words. And since Lee wrote no autobiography, that option was precluded.

So if Lee did not write the words himself, did he speak them . . . for another to record?

We discover the answer in the masterpiece works of General Lee's most famous biographer, Douglas Southall Freeman. Freeman earned the Pulitzer Prize in 1935 for *R. E. Lee: A Biography*, his monumental four-volume tome on Lee.

General Robert E. Lee.
Courtesy of the Library of Congress.

The *New York Times* declared it, "Lee complete for all time."[13] No Civil War buff's library is complete without Freeman's volumes on Lee. Southern to the root, Freeman grew up surrounded by Confederate veterans. Born only two decades after the war's end, and a resident of "Lost Cause" Richmond for most of his life, Freeman was graduated at age 22 from Johns Hopkins with his PhD in history. His passion transferred not into vocation, however, as he worked for 40 years as a newspaper journalist and editor in Richmond, all the while accumulating mounds of historical evidence in support of his research on Lee.

And the research is imposing. In Volume II alone, which includes Antietam, Freeman employs 2,006 footnotes in the course of 563 pages. On some pages, almost every sentence has its own note. Few scholars have matched Freeman's voracious tenacity for sourcing.

"We will make our stand on those hills," appears within a sentence on the opening page of the Antietam chapters.[14] It stands alone as the only quotation on that page, and for that reason, it stands out. Those words reverberate and resonate. In only eight words, Lee paints the scene for Freeman's history.

But who originally documented Lee's line?

Narrative readers of history find source notes distracting. Curious (and skeptical) historians like me enjoy investigating sources. It's my own way of challenging the writers of history, and testing the veracity of their stories. My detective dogma demands distrust; just because it's written doesn't mean it's real. As philosopher Thoreau observed: "The researcher is more memorable than the researched."[15]

Circumstance would suggest that the original documentarian of Lee's eight words knew Lee, understood Lee and stood by Lee on a regular basis—a general perhaps, or a staff officer. No one of this ilk was the recorder. A second guess would include a colonel or some other regimental officer receiving orders for deployment from Lee. Not so. A third option drops us into the ranks. Did General Lee proclaim these words to inspire the troops?

"Morgan. 141." That's our clue—that's the source cited by Freeman. My research revealed William Henry Morgan as the original transcriber of the sentence. Morgan hailed from Campbell County, Virginia, and served in the Clifton Greys, redesignated as Co. C, 11th Virginia Infantry, Kemper's Brigade, D.R. Jones's Division, Army of Northern Virginia. In other words, Morgan's regiment stood with Lee along the Antietam Creek. So far, so good.

I remained unsatisfied. Still driven to see the context of the quotation—beyond the fragment shared by Freeman—I discovered that Morgan had authored a book, entitled: *Personal Reminiscences of the War of 1861-5: In Camp, En Bivouac, on the March, on Picket, on the Skirmish Line, on the Battlefield, and in Prison.* Quite the title! But beware. Morgan's book was not published until 1911, nearly 50 years after Antietam. Could his memory be creating something that never happened?

Sure enough, I found the original passage: "When the head of the column, which was falling back before the Yankee army from the direction of South Mountain, reached a certain point, General Lee remarked, as the troops by his order filed off the road to form line of battle, 'We will make our stand on these hills.'" [16]

Note, Freeman made an error—his quotation read "those" hills. We will forgive him for that.

But can we forgive the sage Southern scholar for overlooking this salient point—*Morgan was not at Antietam.*

How do I know? Morgan himself told me so. In the paragraph preceding his section on Antietam, he wrote that at the end of June 1862 (ten weeks before Antietam): "I went home and remained until restored to health, after a long spell of sickness." Then, later on, in the paragraph following the Antietam description, Morgan informed me: "I rejoined the army near Winchester about the 25th of September, 1862." He returned eight days after the Battle of Antietam.[17]

Since Morgan was not present to hear Lee's words, how could he report them? He wrote, "I have heard some of Company C relate that on the evening of September 15th, when near Sharpsburg [Antietam], they saw General Lee by the roadside."[18] The key word is heard—the story came to Morgan third hand (remember the game "Telephone"?)

So, in sum, the first quoted source Dr. Freeman utilized to establish the dramatic scene at Antietam: 1) originated with a soldier who was not present; 2) who heard the story passed through his comrades; and 3) who wrote about it 50 years later.

How many other "primary" sources are suspect? And in how many other arenas have historians gone off track?

Oh, by the way, I have altered the opening of my battlefield tour.

CHAPTER 6
The Mystery Loser

[S]inners are always more interesting than the saints,
and in real life good people are dismally dull.
Some people seemed to get all sunshine, and some all shadow.
—Louisa May Alcott[19]

CONSIDER ANY PAPER that changed America.

The Declaration of Independence. The Constitution. The Gettysburg Address. The Letter from Birmingham Jail.

Special Orders 191.

Excuse me?

You don't remember this document protected under layers of bullet-proof glass in the National Archives? You don't recall reciting words of inspiration from this? You don't know how this has anything to do with altering America's destiny?

You will recognize, however, the name of the author: Robert E. Lee.

General Lee faced a perplexing problem. He was poised to invade Pennsylvania with his Confederate army, but a United States garrison at Harpers Ferry threatened his advance. Lee worried that the Federals, located to his rear, could sever his supply line, hamper his communications, and perhaps even block his avenue of retreat. These were unacceptable risks, even to a general who accepted risk. Something must be done.

27

So Lee devised a scheme to divide his army, sending two-thirds of his force to surround and capture the U.S. troops at Harpers Ferry.

Lee labeled the plan "Special Orders 191."[20]

"Special" did not mean that General Lee had a particular fondness for these orders. Rather, it indicated a specific action to specific people to conduct a specific mission. The reason "Orders" is plural (spell check keeps correcting and cannot figure this out) is that #191 is one submission in a chronological series of orders. This is the army's way of defying teachers of grammar.

Stranger still than the peculiarity in title is the orders' convoluted journey—the paper ended up in the lost and found department.

It is never good to have instructions misplaced. Then again, most of us purposely rid ourselves of instructions, relying on our instincts to figure it out. But when the instructions are directing an army's movements, and actions (or inactions) determine the fate of nations, the commanders must follow directions. The alternative is, well, unimaginable.

Special Orders 191 required seven different generals to implement seven different directives. If anyone failed to show up at the right place at the right moment, the plan could fail.

The first step in executing the order was its transmission. And here the mystery begins.

An order departing General Lee's headquarters passed through the following sequence. First, a staff officer would summon a courier (with his horse). In this case, numerous couriers, since the order involved seven subordinate generals scattered to all points of the compass. The courier would sign for receipt of the order (accountability), gallop to the recipient's destination, deliver the order, and sign another receipt (more accountability). Note this involves three different hand-changing transactions.

But there is at least a fourth. No courier ever delivered orders directly to the designated general. A staff officer, instead, would receive it, sign for it, and then bring it to the general's attention. A fifth exchange occurred if the staff officer physically delivered the incoming order to the receiving general.

Knowing human nature (and discounting any blame upon the horses), that's five opportunities for breakdown. Times seven (seven generals).

Somewhere along that transmission line, someone lost General Lee's order.

Yet every general appeared in his assigned location and nothing seemed amiss. No one on the Confederate side knew that a copy of Special Orders 191 was missing.

History knows though, because history shows that the "lost orders" arrived in the hands of Lee's opponent, U.S. commander George B. McClellan. Four days after Lee's issuance, McClellan telegraphed President Lincoln: "I have all the plans of the Rebels and will catch them in their own trap."[21]

What happened?

We know that one set of Lee's orders was discovered by an Indiana private and sergeant in a field near Frederick, Maryland. The Hoosiers and their regiment arrived at an abandoned Confederate camp where the men spied a piece of paper in the grass, wrapped around three Southern cigars. Soon the paper (but not the cigars) made its way to McClellan, and the exact location and mission of each of Lee's divisions became known. A discovery unparalleled in U.S. military history!

So who lost the order?

There are several suspects. Confederate General Daniel Harvey Hill seems a likely culprit, as the order was directed to him. But Hill followed the orders precisely—indicating that his copy was delivered to him without incident. So how is this explained? Turns out Hill had received a duplicate set of orders from Stonewall Jackson. Jackson, who assumed Hill was under his command, did not know that Lee had sent a separate order to Hill. Thus, two orders were transmitted to Hill, and Lee's became lost. For the rest of his life, Hill denied ever seeing Lee's order. "My adjutant-general made affidavit, twenty years ago, that no order was received at our office from General Lee."[22]

Perhaps General Hill never witnessed Lee's copy, but what about a member of his staff? All generals have staff officers. Consider this possibility: Jackson's order arrived first, and when Lee's appeared afterward—Special Orders 191 was old news. Thence the staff officer nonchalantly wrapped the paper around three of his cigars and tucked it into his jacket pocket. When the army struck camp and pulled out, in the hustle, the cigars and paper fell out of his pocket, totally unnoticed.

Then there's this possibility. The courier lost the order. Perhaps, when the courier arrived at Hill's headquarters, he received word that General Hill already had these instructions, and that his copy was redundant. The courier was told to keep Lee's copy, and it was never signed for at Hill's headquarters. Before departure, it's reasonable to assume the courier grabbed some food and drink, possibly some rest, and maybe even a fresh horse. At some point, the orders became dislodged, and no one paid attention to the trash on the ground. But how does this explain the cigars? Perhaps the stogies belonged to the courier.

Ever heard the term: "History as Mystery"? One of the principal facts of history is that we often cannot discover the facts. The unknown is more intriguing than the known. Who lost the Lost Order ranks as one of the most fascinating mysteries in American military history. It epitomizes "history as mystery," and is much more interesting and entertaining than history as facts. It also represents how one person, still unknown, can alter the course of history through a mistake.

General Lee's adjutant later Walter H. Taylor commented on the catastrophic outcome of the Lost Order: "The God of battles alone knows what would have occurred but for [this] singular accident. [C]ertainly the loss of this battle order constitutes one of the pivots on which turned the event of the war."[23]

And only God knows . . . who lost the order.

CHAPTER 7

The Villain

Man is the highest product of his own history.
The discoverer finds nothing so grand or tall as himself.
—Theodore Parker[24]

EVERY GOOD STORY requires a villain.

Ancient Rome raged with Caesar versus Brutus. Shakespeare pitted Romeo against Paris. Patrick Henry, of "give me liberty or give me death" fame, vilified King George III. And detective Sherlock Holmes confronted the confounding Professor Moriarty.

Then we have Lincoln versus McClellan.

Wait. Isn't George McClellan working on behalf of Lincoln? Isn't McClellan the U.S. general hand-selected by Lincoln to save the United States?

McClellan, indeed, was Lincoln's chosen savior during the Antietam campaign. But history—and historians— have been unkind to McClellan, portraying him as a character of flaws opposing the preeminent president of character.

I admit my own prejudice against McClellan. I have boisterously bashed the general for decades. I believe he was insubordinate, insufficient, indecisive and inexcusable. Pompous, arrogant, a pouter, neurotic and temperamental, McClellan's personality offends me. We all have known a George McClellan.

I recall engaging in numerous public debates over McClellan with the late Dr. Joseph Harsh, an Antietam aficionado and brilliant scholar whom I admired greatly, except for one thing: Joe admired McClellan. In performances before Civil War audiences, where we verbally tackled one another over the merits and de-merits of McClellan, I always won—not because Joe was an un-equal debater, but because every audience shared a preconceived predilection against McClellan.

McClellan is the Northern Civil War general that Civil War buffs love to hate (Braxton Bragg is bestowed that honor on the South-ern side). What, then, has inspired this loathing?

McClellan himself is a principal source. His own words cause him harm. Fortunately for historians, McClellan's letters to his wife survive, donated by his family to the Library of Congress. Unfor-tunately for McClellan, his personal and private correspondence with his beloved spouse Mary Ellen publicly exposed his flaws. These letters are honest, intimate and unguarded expressions of McClellan's inner soul. No public person ever desires his true self revealed. It's a credit to the McClellan family that they preserved these letters for posterity rather than destroying them to protect personal reputations.

We should offer the McClellan family a meritorious medal. Oh, how our understanding of Little Mac would differ without these epistles. We would not know McClellan's true feelings. We would not know the contents of McClellan's soul. We would not be able to repeat so many of his words (especially those we find so disgust-ing). Consider how rare it is to reach inside a person. Most of us, in fact, create a hard exterior shell labeled "No Trespassing"—pur-posely designed to keep people out. Had McClellan's descendants destroyed his letters (gasp!), we wouldn't know George McClellan, thus ruining careers of many Civil War historians.

But because these documents survived, we discovered McClel-lan's innermost feelings about Lincoln. "What a specimen to be at the head of our affairs now!" McClellan scoffed to Mary Ellen. "He really seems quite incapable of rising to the height of the merits of the question & the magnitude of the crises." Referring to Lincoln's appearance as "the original gorilla" and "an old stick," McClellan considered the president of inferior intelligence, a mindless med-dler, and inept at grasping military matters. McClellan even per-sonalized his disdain for the president: "I can never regard him with other feelings than those of contempt—for his mind, heart & morality."

Maj. Gen. G. B. McCLELLAN & LADY.

George McClellan and wife Mary Ellen Marcy McClellan
Courtesy of the Library of Congress.

McClellan's epithets extended to Lincoln's cabinet as well. "I have lost all regard & respect for the majority of the Administration," he revealed to a confidant, "& doubt the propriety of my brave men's blood being spilled to further the designs of such a set of heartless villains." In an exclamation of rhetoric, he informed Mary Ellen the president and his men had achieved "all that cowardice, folly & rascality can do to ruin our poor country—

& the blind people seem not to see it, but to submit like serfs to the lash."[25]

Oh, my . . . take a breath. Is this any way to speak about our nation's greatest president? (Note: we have 150 plus years of hindsight and a marble memorial in Washington to influence our perspective.)

Historians, too, have prejudiced the public's perception against McClellan. In the three most widely published histories of the Antietam campaign, each historian hurls invectives at General McClellan.

First was Francis Winthrop Palfrey. Palfrey fought at Antietam, serving as lieutenant colonel of the Harvard Regiment (the 20th Massachusetts Infantry). Palfrey himself had graduated from Harvard with a law degree, and as a distinguished son of a Boston abolitionist, educator and congressman. During the fighting in the West Woods, Palfrey was severely wounded, and saved only by a Confederate officer who promised medical attention if he would surrender. Twenty years after the battle, in 1882, Palfrey authored a 135-page monograph on Antietam as part of *Campaigns of the Civil War*—the first mass-public histories about the conflict, published in a stunningly successful Scribner series.

Palfrey did not create the original animus for McClellan. Ample antagonists existed during the war, including Lincoln, his cabinet members, newspaper editors and even fellow officers. But Palfrey's stinging criticisms generated damning and enduring imagery that has condemned McClellan for generations.

"[H]e was not equal to the occasion," Palfrey assessed. "He threw away his best chance, and a precious opportunity for making a great name passed away."

Palfrey's favorite charge against McClellan was, in his judgment, McClellan's propensity for procrastination. "The case called for the utmost exertion, and the utmost speed," Palfrey opined after the Lost Orders came into McClellan's possession. "Not a moment should have been lost . . . It was a case for straining every nerve." Upon arriving along the Antietam Creek, Palfrey condemned McClellan for dithering. "There is no censure too strong for his delay." Exacerbated and exhausted by McClellan's "excuses," Palfrey offered a psychological assessment: "The fault was in the man." [26]

James V. Murfin continued this Palfrey dogma in *The Gleam of Bayonets,* an epic study published in the midst of the wildly popular Civil War Centennial. "McClellan [at Antietam] had the grandest opportunity of his military career," reasoned Murfin. "How he squandered away precious time is a matter of military history and one of the saddest moments of the war for the Union."

I developed my disdain for McClellan through the influence of Jim Murfin. I knew Jim—so well, in fact, that his widow Nancy asked me to deliver a eulogy, representing an aspiring and youthful historian encouraged by and mentored by Jim. I read "The Gleam" over and over again while in school, inspired by Jim's writing and compliant with Jim's conclusions. One of my favorite Murfin musings was this: "Lee invaded Maryland in spite of McClellan; he divided his army in the face of the enemy because of McClellan; he stood at [Antietam] in defiance of McClellan."[27]

Two decades following Murfin's celebrated book, author Stephen W. Sears published *Landscape Turned Red.* Nary a Civil War buff exists who does not possess Sears's volume on Antietam in their personal library. Sears went beyond previous Antietam researchers, however, delving deeply into McClellan's personal papers in an attempt to explain the man.

Like Palfrey and Murfin before him, Sears painted an unflattering portrait. McClellan "lacked the instinct to anticipate and exploit," concluded Sears. The general waddled "in his self-delusion [and] was incapable of understanding." Little Mac (a favorite nickname of the troops) "squandered the unique opportunity of winning a battle of annihilation." Sears concluded McClellan had "lost his inner composure," suffered from "a near paralysis of will," and many of his battlefield decisions were, "for a trained soldier, simply irrational." [28]

How, then, did McClellan ensure the safety of Washington; protect Pennsylvania from invasion, defeat Lee once, and then twice; and run the Rebels out of Maryland?

Is the villain actually the victor?

CHAPTER 8
Here I Am; I Dare You to Stop Me

Forget conventionalism; forget what the world thinks
of your stepping out of your place. [T]hink your best thoughts;
speak your best words; work your best works,
looking to your conscience for approval.
—Susan B. Anthony[29]

CHAOS REIGNED in Washington, D.C.

Robert E. Lee knew the time was ideal for invasion.

The Confederate commander had just completed a remarkable two months. Lee had saved Richmond from capture; befuddled Union generals with daring maneuvers and lightning marches; whipped a Yankee army thirty miles from the U.S. capital; and convincingly cleared occupied Northern Virginia of enemy forces. Lee's bold movements dizzied Federal authorities, now bunkered down behind the defenses of Washington, mired in defeat and demoralization. Northern eyes glowered at Lee, watching for his next audacious move.

They didn't have to stare for long. The first week of September, the Rebel army began splashing across the Potomac River. Invasion!—for the first time spearing into the United States.

Not a single standing bridge crossed the Potomac above Washington, but Lee needed no bridges. The river was shallow—historically low—due to an extended drought during the summer of 1862. River fords once used by Native Americans became clearly visible, presenting Lee with options on where to cross hundreds

Sugarloaf Mountain as illustrated by Civil War artist Alfred Waud.
Courtesy of the Library of Congress.

of cannon, thousands of supply and ordnance wagons (powered by thousands of mules and horses), and tens of thousands of infantrymen.

Then Lee made one of his boldest decisions. He determined the main crossing would occur in full view of, and right under the nose of, a U.S. signal station surveillance post on Sugarloaf Mountain.

What? Display all of your cards at the outset? What kind of strategy is this?

Sugarloaf Mountain can be seen for miles. It towers vertically from nothing, forming an odd, thumb-like geologic formation that looks like a camel's hump. Since the earliest European settlers never viewed such exotic creatures as camels, the mountain reminded them of a nicety found in their kitchens—a sugar loaf (the sweet powder packed into a vertical cone).

From the earliest days of the war, Union observers occupied Sugarloaf's crest, gazing across the Potomac into Loudoun County and Northern Virginia, watching alertly for movements at the edge of the Confederate nation. Sugarloaf, in essence, functioned for the Federals like a spy satellite.

Not only could the Yankees see from Sugarloaf, but they also could communicate. With Sugarloaf clearly visible from Capitol Hill—about 40 miles distant—Union signalmen could wave large flags to transmit coded messages to Washington, aided by magnifying telescopes on tripods. Even at night, the system could work, with fiery torches replacing the flags. Any visible Rebel threat could be relayed to the War Department in moments.

Lee certainly knew of the Sugarloaf surveillance post. It operated with no camouflage, and in easy sight of the Confederates. Conventional military wisdom, therefore, advocated a simple dictate—don't be seen. Avoid enemy detection. A reasonable strategy suggested movement away from Sugarloaf, allowing the invasion force to advance without exposure or encumbrance.

General Lee, instead, defied convention. He enthusiastically embraced exposure. To ensure he would be caught in the act, Lee selected White's Ford as one of his principal crossing points—within the shadow of Sugarloaf. The "Gray Fox" determined to announce his arrival, not disguise it.

Lee wanted the Washington authorities to know exactly where he was. Now in Maryland; now in the North; now leading his army of Rebels into the United States. Vitalized by victories and buoyed by momentum, Lee intended to frighten Washington; threaten Pennsylvania; embarrass the Lincoln Administration; and prove the Confederate army could wage war on foreign (U.S.) soil. Lee expected the Northern electorate to notice his presence, and in eight weeks (in the mid-term elections), to deliver a crushing defeat to the war-leading Republicans. Lee also had diplomacy in mind, hoping with a successful incursion to persuade England and France to recognize the Confederacy as a nation.

For General Lee, launching his invasion in full view of the Sugarloaf signal station was tantamount to announcing the crescendo of Southern independence.

As Lee expected, the Sugarloaf station obliged, sending its first warning at 4 p.m. on September 4. Soon, all regions of the North knew an invasion was underway, and panic alarms sounded. The questions now became, where was Lee headed? How long would he remain? What were his intentions? How do we stop him?

Emboldened by his bloodless border crossing, and confident of continued successes, Lee recommended to his president (Jefferson Davis) that the Confederacy propose ending hostilities. "Such a proposition, coming from us at this time, could in no way be regarded as us suing for peace," Lee determined. "[B]ut, having been made when it is in our power to inflict injury upon our adversary, would show conclusively to the world that our sole object is the establishment of our independence and the attainment of an honorable peace."[30]

Despite this heartfelt hope, Lee anticipated a fight was more realistic than peace. This explained another reason he presented his gambler's hand at Sugarloaf Mountain. The Confederate commander needed to draw the Federals away from the defenses of Washington. Lee knew he did not have the manpower or firepower to strike the most heavily fortified city on earth. If he could lure the Yankees into the field, his odds improved. Lee preferred Pennsylvania as the ring for the titans to wage battle; and as he proceeded north, he desired the Unionists to give chase across the Mason-Dixon Line. When Lee arrived at Frederick, ten miles north of Sugarloaf, he subsequently stopped . . . and waited . . . and watched. How would the enemy respond?

The enemy responded much faster than expected. Just two weeks after initiating his invasion, Lee was in full retreat. Almost none of his aspirations had been fulfilled; two battle defeats had quashed his momentum, and at least one quarter of his army had been killed or wounded.

Perhaps Lee flaunted too much.

CHAPTER 9
Game of Guess

Whatever is almost true is quite false,
and among the most dangerous of errors,
because being so near truth,
it is more likely to lead astray.
—Henry Ward Beecher[31]

IT'S THE OLDEST GAME in human history: "the guess."

The guess is a ubiquitous game. It's everywhere, every day, with everyone. It ceases, it seems, only when we sleep. And when it interrupts our rest and well being, the game of guess becomes stress.

Both guess and stress governed Washington that first week of September in Lincoln's second year as president. An enemy army taunted the generals, tormented the politicians, and tortured the strategists with a consequential guess—a guess that could determine the future of the country.

What was General Lee thinking?

We know. History tells us so. And herein lies a problem with history: We know the end of the story—from the beginning of the story. History opens with the last sentence of the last chapter. We know the final score even as the contest begins. As a result, history reduces the game of guess (fun!), and replaces it with a citation of chronology (boring!).

Let's consider a modern analogy, using another game: football. It's Super Bowl Sunday. Nearly half of America puts their existence on pause as we huddle around our big-screen TV(s) and anxiously await every play. Football, in essence, is a game of guess. We love the suspense; we gorge on the drama. Anticipation builds on every snap. Suddenly, though, too much beer requires we take a break. You scurry off, hoping nothing important happens during your absence. Then from afar you hear yelling and screaming. Oh no. You missed the moment. You return to see the replay—otherwise known as history.

History is a chronological record of occurrences. Some of us enjoy an arranged narrative of happenings, as it brings us order and context and pretext for our existence. But more of us thrive on the haphazard drama of guessing. In other terms, guessing may be defined as options, as alternatives, as choices.

Historians too often disregard—or have little regard for—the game of guess. Instead, they focus upon the decision, or the outcome of the guess. Historians thus start with the end of the story (the outcome), therefore removing the tension and drama and life from the tale. Um-hm, now you understand why you hated your history classes.

Returning to General Lee, let's apply the game of guess to the Confederate commander. Let's begin not with his decisions, but with his options. Lee's location at Frederick, so near the Union capital and so close to Pennsylvania, offered him numerous opportunities. Washington seemed his obvious target. Capture of the enemy's capital defined the ultimate conquest in Napoleonic style warfare. For seventeen months, after all, U.S. strategy had centered upon the capture of Richmond. It seemed apparent that Lee would now turn the tables.

Though the Confederate commander admired risk, he often adopted pragmatism. Lee knew Washington was surrounded by a bulwark of breastworks—fifty fortifications defended by 500 cannon. He recognized as well that more than 150,000 soldiers had assembled in the capital's environs—the largest army on the planet. Despite entreaties from Southern editors to "swallow Washington in one mouthful,"[32] Lee abstained. "I had no intention of attacking [the enemy] in his fortifications," he informed Confederate president Jefferson Davis, "and am not prepared to invest them." [33] Eliminate this option.

Forty miles north of Washington appeared an enticing target—Baltimore. Baltimore was the South's largest city. Force of arms, however, had thwarted Baltimore's unification with the Southern Confederacy. Union authorities had seized the city in the earliest days of the war and had not relinquished it.

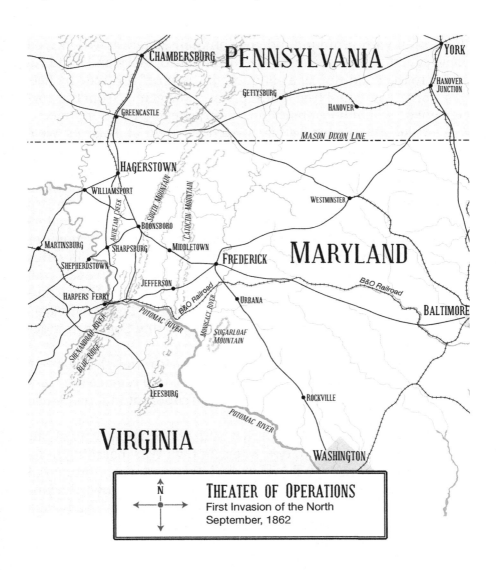

THEATER OF OPERATIONS
First Invasion of the North
September, 1862

Secessionists were arrested, pro-Southern newspapers quashed and earthworks built atop Federal Hill, with cannon aimed at the heart of the city. Worsening matters, to ensure Maryland remained within the United States, Lincoln suspended Constitutional rights throughout the Old Line State and placed the Maryland legislature under house arrest.

Confederates cried foul over these ignominies. Southerners "have seen with profound indignation their Sister State deprived of every right," proclaimed Lee to the people of Maryland, "and reduced to the condition of a conquered province." A rescue by Lee, therefore, that would free Baltimore and Maryland "from this foreign yoke," would boost both moral purpose and Rebel morale.[34]

A strike into Pennsylvania invited positive choices as well. First, from the Confederate perspective, the real invasion of the North would begin once Lee surged across the Mason-Dixon Line. In Pennsylvania resided the genuine enemy. The second most populated state in the North, Pennsylvania had recruited tens of thousands of soldiers who had invaded the South. A preponderance of generals from Pennsylvania wore stars on their shoulder straps. Pennsylvania had contributed manpower from its cities and farms, materials of war from its factories, resources of coal from its mines, and miles and miles of railroads to move men, munitions and machines. Only New York outranked Pennsylvania as the Yankee state most responsible for thwarting Southern independence.

So what better place than Philadelphia to end the war for Southern independence? How fitting if Lee could replace the stars and stripes with the stars and bars on the cupola at Independence Hall.

The distance between Frederick and Philadelphia was about 170 miles—or ten days to two weeks in Civil War marching time. Considering George Washington had tramped his Continental army 680 miles from Newport, Rhode Island, to Yorktown, Virginia, to defeat the British and end the Revolutionary War, an advance upon Philadelphia seemed possible. America's second largest city, without defenses of any sort, believed its capture was "a favorite hope of the Rebels." Philadelphia's mayor minced no words: "The

critical period of the war, as far as the safety of this city is concerned, is now upon us."[35]

The road to Philadelphia passed through Gettysburg. Gettysburg, in fact, would be the first Pennsylvania town Lee would enter if he marched due north from Frederick. A tempting target even further north was Harrisburg, the state capital. How embarrassing it would be to the Union for Lee to start harassing Harrisburg. How would Lincoln and the Republicans explain the collapse of the center of government in the country's second most populous state? "Send here not less than 80,000 disciplined troops," the governor demanded. "The time for decided action by the National Government has arrived. What may we expect?"[36]

General Lee had great expectations, and good options.

Now arrived the moment . . . for his opponents to guess.

CHAPTER 10
Did McClellan Outthink Lee? Part I

*[R]e-examine all you have been told at school or church
or in any book.*
—Walt Whitman[37]

ABRAHAM LINCOLN DID NOT THINK fondly of George McClellan.

The president had just fired his army commander for incessantly demanding more troops, excusing inexplicable delays, crying wolf with inflated enemy numbers and failing to capture the Rebel capital. Lincoln perceived McClellan as overbearing and under-performing, and the persistent man in the White House had lost his patience.[38]

Then cometh the threat of Confederate invasion. Lincoln had no general in charge. He considered his options (none of them promising), and after methodical deliberation, he chose—George McClellan.

"This seemed to me equivalent of making [McClellan] Commander-in-Chief," lamented Salmon P. Chase, Lincoln's treasury secretary. "I could not but feel that giving the command to him was equivalent to giving Washington to the Rebels."[39]

"A terrible and thankless task" was how General McClellan labeled his new assignment. Still smarting from the embarrassment of his firing, and ever scornful of the president, McClellan assumed his new job "reluctantly" and said, "I only consent to take it for my country's sake and with the humble hope that God has called me to it."[40]

God's first task, rightly, would have been to send McClellan Hercules. McClellan inherited a mess. Army officers were charging fellow officers with treason. Loyalties to individuals supplanted loyalty to country. Political parties portrayed their opponents as incompetent and imbecilic. Washington, wandering and wondering, appeared to be sinking in its swamp of paralysis analysis. The emergency within loomed as dangerous as the emergency without.

McClellan applied his greatest strength—organizing control out of chaos—and achieved immediate results. In only four days, he ensured the defenses were manned, the troops mustered, and the army ready to march. Most impressive, McClellan amalgamated the elements of three armies into one, mixing units and commanders that never had united on a battlefield. This included an infusion of tens of thousands of new volunteers, most whom had enlisted within the past three weeks. (No boot camp for these boys—their training would come in the field.)

In addition to the plethora of internal worries, McClellan grappled with the biggest problem of all—Robert E. Lee and his enemy army. As Lee remained static at Frederick watching Washington, McClellan eyed Lee for any hint of Confederate intentions. One red flag waved incessantly before McClellan's brow: Baltimore.

Baltimore was Washington's Achilles heel. Located forty miles north of the capital, Baltimore was the source of the only railroad—repeat, the only railroad—that connected the heart of Union government with the rest of the United States. This artery, if severed, would isolate Washington from the remainder of the country. In more dramatic terms, if the Confederates cut this umbilical cord, Washington would wither.

McClellan knew instinctively, and his military mind confirmed conclusively, that General Lee's logical target was Baltimore—or at minimum, the Washington branch of the Baltimore & Ohio Railroad. This line demanded protection at all hazard. Any move toward Baltimore by the Confederates must be stopped.

The import of this link cannot be overstated. In addition to supplying Washington with essential sustenance such as food and fuel, it offered the lone avenue of rapid transport for troops flooding in from the North. Sever the railroad, and Lee would sever the flow of reinforcements into the capital.

"We can take 28,000 men in one convoy of train from Washington to Baltimore," wired the B&O's president to the secretary of war. Fully understanding the strategic vulnerability of (undefended) Baltimore, the CEO noted he also could transport 2,000 horses and up to 60 pieces of artillery, and could repeat the operation at least once a day. But this came with a warning: "We are not yet advised of any injury whatever to our roads."[41]

This prospect of "injury" (Confederate interruption) became more foreboding as intelligence trickled into McClellan's headquarters. "All reports agree that Baltimore is their destination," deduced McClellan's chief of cavalry, who was collecting information from witnesses within Southern lines. The department commander stationed in Baltimore informed President Lincoln, "Rebels proclaimed that they were going either to Philadelphia or Baltimore." The governor of Pennsylvania learned from his spies: "Received full particulars concerning invasion of Maryland. . . . Announced their destination Baltimore."[42]

McClellan, concerned by this mounting evidence, ordered his first move. He directed his principal thrust north toward Baltimore—not toward Lee at Frederick. He also placed this critical maneuver in the hands of his most experienced subordinate, Ambrose E. Burnside.

Burnside was the only man in McClellan's army of nearly 90,000 men who had commanded an independent army. President Lincoln had such faith in Burnside that he had offered him McClellan's command, not once, but twice (Burnside demurred, favoring McClellan).

The situation became urgent when McClellan received intelligence that both Stonewall Jackson and J.E.B. Stuart—two of Lee's top lieutenants—had moved their headquarters east of Frederick toward Baltimore. "This indicates that enemy intends moving on Baltimore," telegraphed McClellan's headquarters to Burnside. "[I]t is now more necessary than ever that you should promptly execute the instructions."

The instructions were simple—seize the National Road leading to Baltimore and block a hillside gap in central Maryland at a village named Ridgeville. "Should the enemy make any demonstration toward Baltimore ... attack him vigorously," McClellan ordered Burnside. The general then informed the War Department: "They shall not take Baltimore without defeating this army."[43]

No battle occurred; no enemy arrived. Lee instead moved west, away from Baltimore.

■　■　■

GEORGE MCCLELLAN ENSURED the security of Baltimore. His first strategic maneuvers—in the face of an aggressive and unpredictable invader—protected the lifeline feeding Washington. Washington survived this scare, not because of its defenses, but because McClellan defended its most vulnerable point.

Yet historians have given McClellan almost no credit for this feat. Why? Historians have focused the story elsewhere—on McClellan's failure to go after Lee at Frederick, and his reluctance to chase down Lee's army rapidly and expediently. They hurl criticisms of overbearing caution, methodical plodding and glacial movements. Their preconceived prejudices blind their research and fail to reward McClellan for his initial success.

But beneath the veil of the historians' filter is the record; and if you are willing to challenge conventional interpretation, and re-examine the record, it's appropriate to ask:

Did McClellan pilfer from Lee the most valuable prize?

CHAPTER 11

Wrong Guess

Once you make a decision,
the universe conspires to make it happen.
—Ralph Waldo Emerson[44]

HIS NAME IS NOT FAMOUS like Lincoln or Lee.

His moniker hardly befits mention on a second tier of fame, where we find McClellan or Stonewall Jackson or Pierre Gustave Toutant Beauregard (added for its masterful combination of Latin letters that roll off my tongue in a bellicose growl).

Henry Wager Halleck. *Huh?* Reach deep into your gray matter—nothing there. Don't fret. This guy probably never appeared on any of your history tests. And if he did, why remember? (It's okay to admit you don't remember much of anything that concerns history.) Unless you're a hard-core Civil War student, there's an infinitely small chance you've heard of H. W. Halleck.

So who is Halleck? President Lincoln considered him worthy and reliable enough to promote him to "General-in-Chief." An impressive title, fitting for a West Point graduate, so smart that he taught his fellow students while still a cadet at the academy. Halleck eventually became a fine military historian and writer, translating the masterpiece strategy of Antoine-Henri Jomini (Napoleonic war genius) from French into English.

But once Halleck appeared at the War Department—summoned by Lincoln seven weeks before Lee's invasion—the grinder in Washington diminished his reputation from "Old Brains" to "Old Wooden Head." "Halleck originates nothing, anticipates nothing...plans nothing, suggests nothing, is good for nothing," observed Lincoln's secretary of the navy Gideon Welles.[45] Historians enjoy knocking Lincoln for elevating Halleck, considered one of his poorer judgments.

Then again, Lincoln went through seven commanding generals (including McClellan twice) in the eastern theater of the war before he discovered the eventual winner, U.S. Grant.

Halleck possessed power and influence. His principal job, to serve as a master strategist and to coordinate the Union war effort on multiple fronts, was complicated by meddling politicians (including Lincoln) and mercurial generals in the field. Halleck himself often was perceived as micromanaging when he was far afield and ignorant of campaign conditions. He could wield his stick, however, and dictate the rules for, or overrule decisions by, army commanders.

Harpers Ferry was a case in point.[46] When Lee embarked on his invasion, he effectively isolated the Union garrisons at Harpers Ferry and in the Shenandoah Valley. Railroad support was severed, telegraph communication was sliced and assistance through reinforcement nearly impossible.

Given these uncomfortable circumstances, Lee considered untenable the continued presence of U.S. forces in and around Harpers Ferry. "I have no doubt that they will leave that section," Lee informed President Davis on September 5, the second day his army manifestly moved into Northern territory. Lee expected prompt Federal abandonment of the Harpers Ferry sector "as soon as they learn of the movement across the Potomac."

So confident was Lee of this outcome, he sent another message to President Davis two days later: "The Shenandoah Valley has been evacuated."[47]

Lee was wrong. The Bluecoats, indeed, had pulled out of Winchester; but they did not depart the valley. Instead, they joined the garrison at Harpers Ferry, where their combined forces now totaled 14,000 U.S. soldiers, equivalent to an army corps of enemy troops.

Henry Wager Halleck, General-in-Chief.
Courtesy of the Library of Congress.

General Lee was befuddled. This situation failed all good judgment. Why were the Lincolnites lingering? Isolated, seemingly
abandoned, and with no prospect of help, the continued presence
of the Federals about Harpers Ferry confused Lee and generated
not one iota of strategic sense. What were the Yankees thinking?

"Old Brains" Halleck was the conductor of thinking on the
Union side. "Our army in motion," Halleck wired the commander
at Harpers Ferry just before the telegraph went dead. "It is important that Harpers Ferry be held to the latest moment."[48]

George McClellan disagreed. Adamantly. "Colonel Miles [the
commander at Harpers Ferry] can do nothing where he is," clam-
ored McClellan. "I suggest that he be ordered at once to join me
by the most practicable route." In a follow up plea, McClellan
deemed the force defending Harpers Ferry—while posted at the

Ferry—"but [of] little use, and is continually exposed to be cut off by the enemy."[49]

This, precisely, was the common sense response General Lee expected. But Halleck held firmly. "There is no way for Colonel Miles to join you at present," snapped Halleck back at McClellan. "His only chance is to defend his works till you can open communication with him."[50]

Considering the Rebel army at Frederick was wedged between McClellan and Harpers Ferry, Halleck did not offer any recommendations on ways to re-establish this communication. In addition, for General Halleck, communication meant more than a meager telegram or mere courier. His inference was extra challenging—McClellan and his army must conduct a rescue mission for Colonel Miles.

Thus the stage was set for a disaster—but for which side?

■   ■   ■

HISTORIANS HAVE CONDEMNED HALLECK for his determination to hold Harpers Ferry. It's one of the few times, in fact, that historians side with McClellan. Halleck's decision is considered an error of gargantuan proportion, based upon events that soon unfolded.

Yet again, historians formulate these negative opinions through their hindering habit of hindsight. They label Halleck as a bumbler and bungler for his Harpers Ferry decision. They criticize Halleck for incompetence and impertinence. They dramatize Halleck as arrogant and indifferent. They define Halleck as stupid, defying common sense. They censure Halleck for what happened (later on), rather than evaluating Halleck's decision in real time, as it was happening.

Consider this—Halleck's decision to hold Harpers Ferry altered Lee's invasion strategy. Halleck's resolution to retain a Union stronghold at the Ferry stalled Lee's momentum. Halleck's determination to maintain a Federal presence behind Lee's army compelled Lee to counteract. The decision of "Old Brains" Halleck, in essence, frustrated the Confederacy's greatest general at the zenith of the Confederacy. General Lee had guessed wrong.

CHAPTER 12
Brilliant or Baneful?

Fame is a bee
It has a song
It has a sting
Ah, too, it has a wing.
—Emily Dickinson[51]

ROBERT E. LEE was perplexed.

Why were the Yankees still holding Harpers Ferry?

Five days had passed since Lee had inaugurated invasion. From his perch at Frederick, he watched . . . and waited. One eye gazed at Washington. No immediate threat from that quarter. The alternate eye scrutinized the situation at the Ferry, where Lee anticipated—and needed—a Northern withdrawal.

For General Lee, the Federal force at Harpers Ferry was not inconvenient—it was dangerous. It presented a serious obstacle, not before him, but from behind. Worst case scenarios disquieted Lee's mind. The Harpers Ferry garrison could interfere with, or even interrupt, his supply and communications lines to and from Virginia. The enemy could depart the Ferry, spread itself along the Potomac, and block strategic river crossings. Most troubling, perhaps, was the prospect of the Harpers Ferry contingent following Lee northward, pestering him habitually like a swarm of mosquitoes.

As days passed, the steadfastness of the Federals at the Ferry became certain. Frustrated by the Yankees' lack of cooperation,

Harpers Ferry in 1861. Located on the border between North and South, the town would change hands eight times in three years. The stately Baltimore & Ohio Railroad bridge was destroyed eight weeks into the war. *Courtesy of the Harpers Ferry National Historical Park.*

and with his patience exhausted, Lee determined to rid this nuisance from his rear.

Lee's solution: Special Orders 191.[52]

Special Orders 191 had the characteristics of an orchestra composition. Stonewall Jackson, the first chair in the string section, would lead the violins, violas and cellos in a soaring score of surround sound at Harpers Ferry. The brass section, led by Lee and James Longstreet, would remain silent at first, but then modify the music, and trumpet the invasion of Pennsylvania from the stage of the Mason-Dixon Line. Cavalry chieftain J.E.B. Stuart would direct the woodwinds from the back row, scurrying and screening the movements of the army. The percussionists (artillery) were available to punctuate, but their pounding beats still awaited arrangement (if required). Timing—adherence to the clicking metronome—would provide the adhesive that connected each of the notes and each of the sections. And we know the sound of an orchestra that deviates from timing—harmony crashing into unpleasant noise.

Simply stated, Special Orders 191 had one mission—eliminate the U.S. garrison at Harpers Ferry. To accomplish this, Lee directed three separate columns to march upon the Ferry, seizing the three mountains surrounding the Ferry and squeezing the Federals into submission. Once free from this burden, Lee could continue his invasion into Yankee land.

The boldness—the monumental audacity—exhibited by Lee in conceiving and issuing this order was a principal trait that established him as a military genius. Lee's willingness to innovate, and to accept and employ risk, defined his greatness.

But nothing was assured. More so, nothing was simple about the execution of Special Orders 191. Five obstacles could wreck Lee's plan:

Contour
Convergence
Coordination
Communication
Clock

Breakdown opportunities were omnipresent. Two of the columns, for example, had to scale and descend two mountain ranges. Two of the pincers had to re-ford the Potomac River and return to Virginia. The most arduous march (fifty-seven miles) required the ascent and descent of both ridges and the re-crossing of the river. None of this mattered unless the three divergent columns converged at the Ferry at the same time. Then upon arrival, each must seize one of the three heights encircling the town. The Rebel noose hanging from atop the heights never would close if coordination failed amongst the three. Complicating matters, vast separation of the three columns, marching simultaneously from different compass directions, prohibited line-of-sight communication and rendered telegraph transmissions impossible.

Stated simply, you can't see your friends, you can't hear your friends, you can't track your friends. Yet you are expected to show up at the designated place at the appointed time.

Oh, and speaking of time, you have three days . . .

Craziness! you scream at General Lee! (It's okay. You may roar with no fear of insubordination.)

For four decades, I have guided active-duty military officers (including generals) on battlefield tours at Harpers Ferry. Every instance I've described the intricacies of Special Orders 191, they uniformly shake their heads in disbelief. They observe that in today's Army—with modern satellites, cellular phones, GPS coordinates and lightning mobility—they probably would fail the provisions set forth in S.O. 191.

Robert E. Lee, however, believed it doable, and success probable. Pause for a moment. Re-read, slowly, the difficulties inherent in the execution of these orders.

Consider these questions. Was Lee too confident? Did he suffer from the self-delusion of the super-strength of his army? Had Lee become careless?

And within this volcano of improbabilities, not one word has yet been mentioned about the biggest unknown of all—the response of the enemy.

Lee seemed unconcerned. Though he was splitting his army into four segments (three en route to Harpers Ferry), Lee felt certain his detachments would conquer the Ferry and reunite before any encounter with the U.S. army based in Washington. Enemy commander McClellan, for the moment, appeared more focused on defensive maneuvers (true) to protect Baltimore and the capital than chasing after Lee. But one glance at the map showed McClellan could race to Harpers Ferry in three days—equal to the time Lee was allotting for the enactment of Special Orders 191. This posed potential for collision. Lee, apparently, dismissed this possibility. He judged, instead, that he had the time necessary to reduce Harpers Ferry without menace.

Stonewall Jackson agreed and enthusiastically endorsed the scheme. Lee assigned him control over the Harpers Ferry mission. James Longstreet, on the other hand, disagreed. "I objected," declared Longstreet. "[I]t would be a bad idea to divide our forces while we were in the enemy's country."[53]

Stop! Was it acceptable for Longstreet to challenge Lee? Yes. General Lee would have expected his trusted lieutenant to offer his opinion. But Longstreet wrote those words in the mid 1880s— more than two decades after Lee issued the orders—in an article included in the "The Century War Series" for *The Century Magazine.* Longstreet had more than 20 years to think about his response.

And here's my knock against historians. Time and again, historians have quoted Longstreet as the curmudgeon holding out against Lee's bold plan. Really? What contemporary evidence—in September, 1862—reveals Longstreet's objection? Nothing. I'm sharing Longstreet's quote, as I want you to judge its veracity. But beware. Don't be gullible. Be especially skeptical of reminiscences. Do not accept them as truth.

Returning to General Lee and his minimization of risks with Special Orders 191, in addition to downplaying the Five Cs (see above) and perceiving no threat from McClellan and the U.S. forces about Washington, General Lee made one other significant assumption—the enemy at Harpers Ferry would succumb without a fight.

Bad assumption.

CHAPTER 13
Until the Cows' Tails Drop Off

One would like to be grand and heroic, if one could;
but if not, why try at all?
—Harriett Beecher Stowe[54]

DIXON MILES KNEW they were coming.

The commanding officer at Harpers Ferry didn't know an iota about Special Orders 191, but from the aggressive movements of the Confederates, he surmised he was the Rebels' bulls-eye.

Colonel Miles also understood he was alone. With no telegraphic communications and no way to connect with U.S. forces, Miles stood by himself as the Rebel tsunami approached.

And run? Not an option. "[B]e energetic and active, and defend all places to the last extremity," ordered Miles's commander in Baltimore. Then followed this emphatic emphasis: "There must be no abandoning of post, and shoot the first man that thinks of it."[55]

Dixon Stansbury Miles did not fear the Confederates. A West Point graduate and a forty-two-year veteran of military service, Miles, in the antebellum army, outranked Robert E. Lee and virtually every other officer who had become a Civil War general. His reputation, unfortunately, had been damaged in the first battle of the war (he was accused of drunkenness at Bull Run). Thus, instead of rising in rank and distinction in battle, McClellan assigned him an administrator's function at Harpers Ferry, where he commanded the "Railroad Brigade."[56]

Well, this was Miles's chance to redeem himself. Lee's invasion shined center spotlight upon Harpers Ferry. But the impending fight would not be fair. Miles would be outnumbered two to one—one of the few times Confederate strength was superior to the Federals. Just as bad, Miles did not have seasoned troops to battle Lee's veterans. Two of every three men under Miles's command—two thirds of his force—had never seen a Rebel, never shot at a Rebel and never been fired upon by Rebels. As new recruits, just enlisted in response to President Lincoln's call for volunteers, many of Miles's men had worn an Army uniform for all of three weeks.

But Miles no longer could fret about his "fortified camp of instruction." He needed to prepare for self defense.

Fortunately, he had a good model. One hundred days earlier, Stonewall Jackson had threatened Harpers Ferry during the outset of his famous Shenandoah Valley Campaign. But Jackson failed to dislodge the Yankees (the only place where they didn't evacuate and run). Miles, who witnessed this defense, determined to duplicate it.

Three mountains surround Harpers Ferry, enclosing the town within a triangle. Maryland Heights, the tallest, was an obvious choice for deployment. Bolivar Heights, the smallest, stood guard over approaches from the Shenandoah Valley. Miles was aware the largest enemy force was approaching from the Valley, so he arranged the bulk of his infantry and artillery atop Bolivar Heights. The third mountain, Loudoun Heights, Miles decided to ignore. Why? The colonel reasoned the Confederates could not reach him from there. A steep vertical drop from the mountain top, combined with the moat of the Shenandoah River at its base, blocked passage from Loudoun Heights; and besides, the mountain was too distant for the range of enemy rifle fire.[57]

Maryland Heights was the key to everything. As a West Pointer with four decades of military experience, Miles understood he must hold the high ground.[58]

Robert E. Lee understood the same. Lee remembered well the topography of Harpers Ferry, as he had been there supervising the capture of John Brown three years earlier.

Colonel Dixon S. Miles
Courtesy of the Library of Congress.

Special Orders 191 specifically targeted Maryland Heights. "So long as Maryland Heights was occupied by the enemy," observed Lafayette McLaws (the Confederate general Lee charged with seizing this position), "Harpers Ferry could never be occupied by us."[59] The stage was set for collision. Few realize it, but the first infantry battle in Maryland during the Civil War occurred on Maryland Heights.

The farmers in nearby Pleasant Valley were awakened at dawn on September 13, 1862, by crackling and snapping sounds never heard before. Confederates from South Carolina and Mississippi had crept up the mountain the previous night and opened fire at sun's first light. U.S. soldiers from Ohio, New York and Maryland promptly unleashed a hailstorm of bullets. Plumes of powder smoke arose from the Elk Ridge mountaintop just north of Maryland Heights, appearing as an inferno. The fight for Harpers Ferry had commenced.

Buffered behind breastworks of logs, the Federals held. Only one hundred yards separated Union defenders from Confederate attackers. The South Carolina commander reported "a most obstinate resistance" and "a fierce fire."[60] For four hours, the boulder-strewn crest, with merely the length of a football field separating enemies, was the deadliest place in America.

Then, suddenly, chaos—a rookie regiment from New York, holding the Union center, collapsed when its colonel was shot in the jaw. The regiment panicked. The Federal line bent, then cracked, then broke.[61] After much effort, it reformed one quarter mile south toward the Ferry, still clinging to the crest. Many of the frightened rookies, however, skedaddled down the mountain, where they encountered Colonel Miles.

Miles had just arrived. A scene of confusion, even pandemonium, greeted the grizzled veteran as the raw recruits scurried about the brigade headquarters, located about half way up the mountain. Using his sword as a club and bolstered by a vent of vernacular (that would guarantee a mouth-wash of soap from any pious mother), Miles restored order. Then he received good news—the majority of his men had not fled, and still retained a strong position on the crest. Miles ordered the brigade commander to stand firmly.[62] He then galloped back into the Ferry to deal with emergencies elsewhere—more Confederates were arriving.

Soon written pleas from the Maryland Heights commander arrived, begging for permission to retreat. This perplexed Miles. The mountaintop was quiet for the moment; from what he could ascertain, his troops held steady.

Certain the loss of Maryland Heights would prove suicidal, Miles transmitted this order: "Since I returned to this side, on close inspection I find your position more defensible than it appears when at your station." Retreat would not be an option, Miles said, adding: "[Y]ou will hold on, and can hold on, until the cows' tails drop off."[63]

Afternoon arrived. Rebels, ignoring the natural obstacles, had seized Loudoun Heights. They had cornered Union troops on Bolivar Heights. Maryland Heights, mysteriously, remained tranquil—until about 3:30 p.m. Then it happened. No gunshots shattered the peace. An astonishing scene, instead, underscored the moment—a long blue line of Federal troops was slithering down the slope in retreat.

"God almighty!" exclaimed an exasperated Colonel Miles. "What does that mean? They are coming down! Hell and damnation! They are coming down!"[64]

Had the cows' tails dropped?

CHAPTER 14
Stonewall Stalled

History, like love, is so apt to surround her heroes
with an atmosphere of imaginary brightness.
—James Fenimore Cooper[65]

SPEED. STEALTH. STEADFASTNESS.

Stonewall Jackson had mastered these traits and earned an incomparable reputation. Second only to Robert E. Lee, Jackson had become the most famous general in the Confederacy.

Jackson's aggressiveness and dexterous skills chiseled him as the ideal partner for implementation of Lee's innovative, and often risky, strategies. Jackson eagerly accepted challenge and thrived on achieving the nearly impossible.

So when he arrived late at Harpers Ferry, something was amiss. Tardiness was not a Jacksonian characteristic.

Stonewall was behind schedule. It was Saturday, September 13. He was approaching Harpers Ferry as directed in Special Orders 191—but he had missed the deadline. The orders called for the completion of the Harpers Ferry mission by September 12. Jackson not only was a day late in finishing the job, he was just beginning.

No deficiency in Jackson's alacrity caused the delay. Stonewall had marched his men nearly 60 miles in three days, typical of his "Foot Cavalry." His troops had tramped up and down Catoctin

Thomas Jonathan "Stonewall" Jackson.
Courtesy of the National Archives.

Mountain near Frederick; then repeated the trial again at South Mountain near Boonsboro. Then they re-crossed the Potomac using a ford at Williamsport, returning to Virginia, where they promptly charged toward Martinsburg, chasing the Yankees there into the trap that was about to snap at the Ferry. By itself, this circuitous trek was impressive.[66] But the march was not the mission.

Lee and Jackson had miscalculated. They erred in judging the amount of time required to reach Harpers Ferry. They overestimated their ability to overcome the barriers of terrain and the distance of geography. That which they deemed possible had proven impossible.

Jackson, however, was not alone in his tardiness. Lee's instructions to seize Maryland Heights and Loudoun Heights also were not realized until September 13th. The entire operation was off schedule.

Good news, though—each of the three separate columns had arrived almost simultaneously. Despite difficulties with communication and coordination, the convergence had worked. Each edge of the Rebel triangle—moving from three different directions toward three separate targets—had turned up together to ensnare the Federals at the Ferry—miraculous, almost, considering the complexity of the maneuver.[67]

What harm, then, was caused by the delay?

Serious harm, in fact. McClellan had moved! (Note: many Civil War buffs consider this an oxymoron.)

The Union commander had departed the defenses of Washington and concentrated his army at Frederick much sooner than anticipated. This was unexpected. Lee had miscalculated. The Federals had drawn too close for comfort. Only 20 miles—a good day's march—now separated McClellan from Harpers Ferry.

Had Special Orders 191 been completed on time, however, McClellan's presence would matter little. If Jackson had been on schedule, the Harpers Ferry mission would have concluded, Lee's fragmented and scattered army reunited and the Confederates would have been en route to Pennsylvania well before McClellan floated into Frederick. The problematic timeline in Special Orders 191, therefore, portended paralyzing problems.

Jackson's immediate trouble, though, was not McClellan. It was Colonel Miles. When conceiving Special Orders 191, Lee anticipated little, and perhaps no defense of Harpers Ferry by the Unionists. He determined that once surrounded, Miles would yield. There would be no investment, no reason for a siege. Miles would quit, and that would terminate the bit.

Lee had miscalculated yet again. Miles waged battle atop Maryland Heights, delaying the Confederate operation for a day on September 13. He then concentrated his force on Bolivar Heights, and engaged in a stare-down with Jackson, about one mile distant on

School House Ridge. Miles's situation, indeed, was desperate. He was encircled; he had lost advantage of the high ground on Maryland Heights; he was isolated and had no communication with allies; and he was outnumbered twice over. Despite all of these disadvantages, Miles stood firmly and prepared to hold Harpers Ferry "until the last extremity."[68]

Frustrated by Miles's resolve, Jackson unexpectedly discovered himself preparing for a siege operation. Confounding! This was not the plan. Lee's original intent was to go in and get out. Union resistance was not predicted. More time expended; more time lost.

Another problem now jolted Jackson—choreography. His force was divided into three columns that were occupying three mountains separated by two rivers (the Potomac and Shenandoah), with an enemy army in the middle of it all. A siege at Harpers Ferry required the same components as the maneuver to Harpers Ferry—communication, coordination and convergence. To ensure the three C's, Jackson first attempted dialogue, via signal flags, with his detachments on Maryland and Loudoun Heights. This failed. Old Jack then reverted to the backup, dispatching couriers who were required to gallop long distances over rough terrain. Aggravated, Jackson admitted on the evening of the 13th: "Before the necessary orders were thus transmitted, the day was far advanced."[69]

Worse still for Jackson, was his tactical dilemma. How did he envision dislodging the stubborn Yankees? Artillery—deploy the guns!

This solution likely made Jackson's heart pulsate. Sixteen years earlier, on the same day, September 13th, Jackson had wheeled his two cannon into the throat of the Mexican defenders in the Battle of Chapultepec, helping ensure victory for the American army and the subsequent fall of Mexico City. The feat earned Jackson honor and distinction and a prompt promotion to brevet major. Later as a professor at the Virginia Military Institute, Jackson taught the cadets the art of artillery. Artillery, determined Jackson, would carry the day at Harpers Ferry.

But not on this day. Night had arrived on the 13th without a piece of artillery in position. And here, Jackson encountered a serious impediment—mountaintops. Maryland Heights soared

1,100 feet above Harpers Ferry, and the vertical walls of Loudoun Heights, 900 feet above the town. It seemed improbable, nay impossible, to drag 2,000-pound cannon up those steep slopes. Colonel Miles, in fact, had determined his defense on the inability of the enemy to post cannon atop those heights.

Stonewall Jackson had defined his Civil War career by meeting challenges. He would defeat the doubters. Orders subsequently circulated to the detached commanders to position cannon on the crests. Jackson dared the mountains to beat him.

But his clock was ticking against him.

CHAPTER 15

Dark Shadows

*One does not see his thought distinctly
till it is reflected in the image of another's.*
—Bronson Alcott[70]

GENERAL LEE WAS EXPECTING a good day.

As dawn arrived on Saturday, September 13, the Confederate commander gazed northward from his Hagerstown headquarters. Pennsylvania was in sight, only five miles distant. Lee, in fact, had already dispatched troops to the village of Middleburg, straddling the famous Mason-Dixon Line.[71] The Confederacy's moment had arrived. Invasion of the real North was imminent.

Pennsylvania had been Lee's destination from the outset. Nine days earlier, on the eve of sending his army across the Potomac, Lee had telegraphed his president, Jefferson Davis: "Should the results of the expedition justify it, I propose to enter Pennsylvania."[72] The entrance, now, was before him—and wide open.

But Lee could not yet press the invasion button. Jackson was away with two-thirds of the army, 28 miles south at Harpers Ferry. Lee expected that mission to conclude expeditiously, however, and his scattered forces to reunite in short order. Today, perhaps, would be the day.

As Lee waited patiently for Stonewall's return, Pennsylvania panicked. "If ever an opportunity was afforded you to prove your love of country, the present hour supplies it," pleaded Pennsylvania's governor, begging for thousands of militiamen to turn out and defend the Quaker State. "The enemy is at your very door . . . For God's sake, arouse from your lethargy before it is too late."[73]

With Lee at the gateway into Pennsylvania's rich Cumberland Valley, the governor and most of his constituents were scared. Convinced the Confederates would seek vengeance for the horrors of war inflicted upon their Southern homeland, the governor warned his people: "We begin now to realize that our own valleys and riversides may be made the scene of the conflict; that instead of invaders, we are to become the invaded; that flame, and pillage, and slaughter, which have wasted distant regions [is coming] upon the peaceful fields and around the quiet homes of our own State." The governor concluded with an abysmal prediction: "This may be the final ordeal through which it may be ours to pass."[74]

Without setting foot into Pennsylvania, Lee was achieving results. The Quakers were quaking; the Stock Market was plummeting; newspaper editors were casting dismal projections; and the Lincoln Administration appeared incompetent and imbecilic. Every day Lee spent threatening the North equated to votes against the Republicans and the war's continuance. Psychologically, Lee was achieving his expectations. Now was the time for the sequel—military invasion.

But where was Jackson? Lee was becoming worried. Reverberations of thunder began echoing off of distant mountains to the south, but not thunder of the heavenly type. Cannon! What was happening at Harpers Ferry?

Lee had learned Jackson was behind schedule. The cannon roar from Maryland Heights aroused anxiety. Lee particularly became concerned for the command of General Lafayette McLaws, whom he directed in Special Orders 191 to seize Maryland Heights and barricade Harpers Ferry from the north. "General Lee desires me to say that he has not heard from you since you left the main body of the army [three days ago]," scribbled Lee's military secretary in a courier message to McLaws on September 13. "He is anxious that the object of your expedition be speedily accomplished."[75]

McLaws did not respond. Meanwhile, the situation worsened. Late that afternoon, Lee received reports that the U.S. cavalry had seized Braddock Gap in the Catoctin range, just west of Frederick.

This unexpected and unwelcome news meant that McClellan had removed the cork on the funnel. With the Catoctins breached, a barrier between Lee and the enemy had burst. Lee knew his next bulwark (South Mountain) was ill-protected, as he never expected a Yankee threat in that quarter. If the Federals poured over South Mountain, Lee himself faced grave danger at Hagerstown, with his flank insecure and his line of retreat threatened.

The severity of these alarms became apparent later that evening. Lee received confirmation of his worst scenario. Union infantry, too, was crossing the Catoctin. Only nineteen miles stood between McClellan's front at Middletown and Lee's location at Hagerstown. Unacceptable, and unbearable.

General Lafayette McLaws.
Courtesy of the Library of Congress.

Lee looked squarely at the facts—his strategic situation was deteriorating . . . rapidly. So bad, in fact, that he decided to abandon his Mason-Dixon Line front.

Parting from the portal into Pennsylvania must have been one of the most painful decisions of Lee's life. Momentum was his. The Confederacy's strength was at a crescendo. Prospects for peace, through the strength of invasion, appeared possible. But peace, and the invasion, must wait. Preserving the army was his first priority.

About two hours before midnight, Lee began withdrawing away from Pennsylvania and Hagerstown. He determined eventually to concentrate at South Mountain, reinforcing a rear guard there. Lee hoped he could seal the mountain's gaps and prevent further advance by McClellan. This meant battle! Lee didn't intend to fight here; he didn't desire to fight here. But he had no choice. Jackson's debilitating delay at Harpers Ferry had hurled an anchor overboard from Lee's flagship. The invading fleet had stalled, and perhaps even stopped.

Still hearing nothing from General McLaws, Lee knew nothing of his battle victory earlier that day atop Maryland Heights. Such good news may have relieved Lee of anxiety and promised encouragement from otherwise discouraging delays. Instead, Lee had received yet more daunting news from his omnipresent scouts. In his final message of a frustrating day, Lee warned McLaws: "[I believe] the enemy is moving toward Harpers Ferry to relieve the force they have there." Most hazardous. Beware. Aware that McLaws—in his isolated and vulnerable position north of the Ferry—would be the first U.S. target, Lee sent him a siren alert: "You will see, therefore, the necessity of expediting your operations as much as possible." [76]

The invasion was unraveling. The army switching from offense to defense. The night was descending into a nightmare for R. E. Lee.

It had been a bad day. The morrow would be even worse.

CHAPTER 16
Trash Talk

Originality is simply a pair of fresh eyes.
—Thomas Wentworth Higginson[77]

WE DON'T KNOW WHO LOST Special Orders 191, but we know who found it.

Two Hoosiers were looking for a place to settle. They just had arrived on the outskirts of Frederick with their regiment (the 27th Indiana Infantry) after an early morning march. As the September sun was beginning to sizzle, they spied a lonely locust tree casting shade in a wheat field. As they neared the tree, they spotted some throwaway trash on the ground—an envelope.

It was not unusual, in fact expected, to find litter (and lice) in an abandoned Confederate encampment. Curious, though, Corporal Barton Mitchell stooped to investigate. As he picked up the Rebel rubbish, a pleasant surprise—out popped three Southern cigars—quite a find, as they were fresh and dry, and apparently dropped only recently.[78]

Given human nature, and the plethora of options bombarding us daily, consider scenarios that might have happened next (the alternate universe theory). Mitchell keeps the cigars and throws the envelope away. Or Mitchell uses the envelope to start a cooking fire (food always is on the mind). Or Mitchell never opens the envelope to discover its inner contents, discarding the paper with a pitch, returning it to trash.

Or what if Mitchell was illiterate? Pause on that notion . . . the words might as well be hieroglyphics. No problem, however. His accomplice, Sergeant John Bloss, was the regiment's only college graduate. Bloss, then serving as second in command of his platoon and used to reading orders, noticed something peculiar about this rubbish—it looked like orders.

Yet again we must consider the human dimension. What if Bloss reads the order, judges it a hoax, and ditches the paper? Or he decides this is a nice war souvenir, and he folds it into his blanket roll to send home later. Or he's the smoker, and he uses the order as a lighter.

None of the above scenarios occurred. The two men knew they had discovered something special in Special Orders 191. But consider how history would have changed—through the casual course of human decision—if Mitchell or Bloss had selected any other perfectly natural option.

Though the two Midwesterners correctly assessed the paper's potential, it was not their role to interpret its meaning nor alter the direction of an army. Anywhere up the chain of command, its progressions could have ceased. And it's a long chain from Mitchell to McClellan. Consider how many officers examined this paper, each performing his duty and accepting his responsibility. First, it arrives in the hands of company commander Captain Kop. Is this genuine? Then up to regimental commander Colonel Colgrove. Is this a ruse? Then it is forwarded to brigade headquarters and General Gordon. Isn't this too obvious? Then it pushes on to division command and General Williams. Is this a trap?

Any of these officers—just one—could have halted the orders' progress to McClellan's headquarters. No one blocked it. Considering the nature of military officers—always inquisitive and sometimes conservative—it's unnatural that natural human instinct didn't stop it. The miracle of Special Orders 191 is not in its discovery, but in its elevation. A piece of trash, literally, leaped up a ladder of bureaucracy into the hands of the army's top commander.

"I think Lee has made a gross mistake," an exuberant McClellan informed President Lincoln. "I have all the plans of the Rebels and will catch them in their own trap . . . Will send you trophies."[79]

Poor McClellan. His own enthusiasm would condemn him. Never mind that he compelled Lee to abandon his Pennsylvania invasion. Ignore McClellan's movements that forced Lee into an unwanted fight and an unimaginable battlefield retreat. These were not "trophies," based upon the bar of standards established for McClellan by historians—a bar that measured success only with the extinction of Lee's army.

Leading historians have defined "trap" differently for McClellan. Little Mac's paid the price in tarnished reputation ever since. For example, to "catch them," historians gave McClellan no credit for moving his forces to intercept Lee's scattered divisions. The historical narrative, instead, concentrated on delays. Other instances of McClellan's actions also received no attention. To stop them, McClellan issued specific orders on relieving beleaguered Harpers Ferry. To disrupt them, Little Mac directed his cavalry to be aggressive and omnipresent, clearing the way over the Catoctin range, and pointing a spear toward the Confederate heart. To infiltrate them, McClellan ordered Burnside's troops on a night march (not typical) to hasten the seizure of South Mountain.[80]

The initial consequence of McClellan's actions—the Rebels noticed. So much so that it forced Lee to draw away from Pennsylvania and altered his plans for continuance of the invasion.

No matter these achievements, historians have castigated McClellan for failing to move, charging him with inaction and derelict delay.

"A full eighteen hours would pass before the first Yankee soldiers marched in response to the discovery," claimed Stephen Sears in *Landscape Turned Red*, the most popular book on the Antietam Campaign.[81]

This charge is spurious—downright false. Sears's apparent disgust and distaste for McClellan (shared by me for years) selected only one bit of evidence to justify this claim, ignoring a preponderance of proof to the contrary. The one shred of evidence: a 6:20 p.m. missive to a subordinate general to move against Harpers Ferry the next morning (September 14). "No doubt had the situation been reversed and a Lost Order presented to Robert E. Lee," opined Sears, "that general would have had Jackson's foot cavalry

Special Orders 191, the copy discovered at Frederick and delivered to General McClellan. Original located within the papers of General McClellan at the Library of Congress.
Courtesy of the Library of Congress.

on the march within the hour and every other man in his arm who could carry a rifle moving after them within two."[82]

McClellan had his faults. I, for one, have pounded him for decades. He did have a bad reputation for slowness, and deserved, due to his preparation and deliberateness in the campaign to take Richmond. But that was a spring and summer ago. The situation in September was entirely different. The U.S. capital was at risk, Northern territory invaded, and the very future of the Union at stake. Was it impossible for McClellan to rise above his flaws and scrap his past bad habits to respond to the current emergency?

Apparently so, according to numerous histories of the campaign.

The principal charge concerned the fault of "delay." Most historians projected this failing onto the Lost Order scenario. McClellan waited (according to historians' doctrine), despite his grand find, wasting precious hours that saved Lee from destruction.

I used to preach from that pulpit. But after years of study—and my own evolution in thought—I have changed. This argument is specious: "Opinion can be so perverted as to cause the false to seem the true."[83]

Sears's notion that McClellan delayed 18 hours was a generated falsehood. To sustain the doctrine of delay, Sears chose to ignore obvious evidence otherwise. On the afternoon of September 13, soon after McClellan's receipt of the Lost Order, Little Mac had his army in motion—moving from Frederick toward Lee—on the most direct path toward Lee's vulnerable mid-section. Sears's assertion that "no Federal troops stirred from their camps that day," defied the known facts, apparently to cause prejudice against McClellan.

Confederates themselves are the best refutation of Sears's allegation. Confirmation of McClellan's aggressive movements came from Rebel reports and Rebel responses. Lee reacted to an unexpected emergency. "[McClellan] immediately began to push forward rapidly," reported the Southern commander.[84] Note Lee's words: "immediately" and "rapidly." Whom do you believe—Lee or Sears?

Lee's man protecting his rear—that was quickly changing into his front—also verified the sudden Union advances. "The enemy soon appeared in force crossing the mountain," cavalry chieftain

J.E.B. Stuart reported about action on the afternoon of September 13.[85] Note Stuart's language: the time was "soon"; the strength, "in force," (i.e., impressive); the action was "crossing." The mountain referred to by Stuart was the Catoctin at Braddock Gap, located nearly six miles west of Frederick. Stuart's evidence, by itself, refuted Sears's false assertion that "no Federal troops stirred from their camps that day."

Beware history . . . and tendencies toward trash talk.

CHAPTER 17
Fortune or Misfortune

We too often bind ourselves by authorities
rather than by truth.
—Lucretia Mott[86]

PERHAPS NOTHING IN ANTIETAM LORE generates more discussion than Special Orders 191.

When I ask Civil War buffs to name for me one order, any order—by name—issued during the Civil War, or any war, the chorus responds "191." It's a badge of honor for aficionados to report on the order's details, in all its complexity, defining the movements, identifying the targets, and characterizing the roles and responsibilities of the players.

Then follows the controversy. No single order of the Civil War has generated more decibels of debate. As a number, it literally is routine and meaningless excreta. But as human drama, it captivates us; it motivates us to explore history as a progression from dilemma to choices, then decision to consequences. We relate well to the story of 191, because it reflects the foibles and fallacies and frailness of our own journeys through life.

General Lee, we challenge first. Did he take too much risk? Was he too confident, perhaps even arrogant, in overestimating his capabilities and underestimating his enemies? Did he adjust and reveal flexibility when his plans unraveled? In his emergency, did he

General George Brinton McClellan.
Courtesy of the Library of Congress.

panic, or respond with measured deliberateness and authority? Such queries we pose to ourselves, replacing he with "I" and his with "my."

The protagonist in the story of Special Orders 191 is General Lee. Historians portray Lee as the heroic figure who overcomes his adversity and conquers his adversary.

The story's antagonist is George B. McClellan. Calculating and cautious, contentious and contemptible, conceited and controversial, few Civil War historians or buffs defend or stand beside Little Mac. In a culture that deifies the Big Mac, how can a self-respecting student of the war belittle oneself?

The charges levied against McClellan in the historian's court are: 1) exaggeration of enemy strength; 2) incessant demand for reinforcements to neutralize his opponent's imaginary numbers;

3) paralysis analysis due to methodical preparation and ad infinitum planning; 4) slow and deliberate movement, if movement at all; 5) excessive caution and abhorrence of risk; and 6) perfection—impossible to attain—but McClellan's standard. This indictment excludes his character flaws, something that is not necessary here for conviction.

Historians have judged and passed their verdict—guilty on all charges. The sentence—permanent abhorrence of all matters McClellan.

In the story of Special Orders 191, McClellan is the favorite foil (and fool) to Lee. Through miraculous good fortune, Lee's Lost Order falls into McClellan's hands. Hereafter, though, historians present McClellan as a cascade of failures. He fails to move rapidly upon receipt of the enemy's plans. He fails to exploit the separation in Lee's army, spending too much time thinking rather than acting. He fails to relieve besieged Harpers Ferry. He fails to crush Lee at South Mountain. And ... drum roll ... he fails to destroy the Confederate Army and end the war there and then.

I, myself, have accepted these precepts, schooled by my mentors, Palfrey, Murfin and Sears (the anti-McClellan firm).

Palfrey established the mash-and-mush McClellan foundation in his Antietam treatise—the first monumental work on the campaign, published in 1882 by Scribner's in its highly popular *Campaigns of the Civil War* series. "The case called for the utmost exertion, and the utmost speed," Palfrey argued. "[N]ot a moment should have been lost in pushing his columns ... It was a case for straining every nerve."

If that doesn't paint a permanent picture of frozen ice in your mind, Palfrey continued his critique: "It cannot be said that McClellan did not act with considerable energy, but he did not act with sufficient." Palfrey smashed his grand slam with this: "The opportunity came within his reach, such an opportunity as hardly ever presented itself ... and he almost grasped it, but not quite."[87]

Some eighty years passed before the Antietam Campaign again splashed as a subject of a popular history. James Murfin's *The Gleam of Bayonets*, published in 1964 by respected New York publisher A. R. Barnes & Co., widely circulated during the euphoria of the Civil War Centennial. It became the standard volume on Antietam, accepted by most scholars and consumed as gospel by the Civil War community (including me).

Palfrey exercised a significant influence upon Murfin and fed his anti-McClellan views. "There can be found no plausible reason for McClellan's delay in moving . . . immediately upon receipt of the [Lost Order]," Murfin editorialized. "His most fervent supporters can offer no excuse for such negligence."

Negligence is a damning word. It resonates long after it's read. Murfin, in his book and in lectures he delivered (and that I eagerly heard), enjoyed quoting the observation of Kenneth Williams, a severe McClellan critic. "It is to be hoped that some capable smokers derived more good out of the three cigars than McClellan was to get out of the order in which they were wrapped."[88]

The grand champion of McClellan criticism goes to Stephen Sears. No human alive has spent more time with McClellan than Sears. He sacrificed several years plowing through McClellan's voluminous archives at the Library of Congress, and served all historians well with his published work excerpting McClellan's papers. Sears's volume on the Antietam Campaign is the most successful book on the subject in history, with tens of thousands of copies sold. Countless times, when I am commencing a battlefield tour or delivering a lecture, audience members have waved their *Landscape Turned Red* like a green flag. Sears also produced a separate volume, a biography exclusively about McClellan.

None of these works flatter McClellan. Each of them presents McClellan as despicable. With regard to McClellan and the opportunities presented by Special Orders 191, he opines: "[H]e geared all his plans to reducing the risk to his own army to a minimum . . . to strike ruthlessly and suddenly for the jugular; to seek to win it all at a stroke—and with it most likely the war—would be to gamble, and a messiah could not afford to be a gambler."[89]

McClellan himself is the source of much of the invective hurled against him. He did exaggerate enemy numbers. He did ceaselessly call for reinforcements. He did plan persistently. He did move methodically. He did exercise caution. He did refrain from risk. He did strive for perfection. In other words, McClellan exercised his rights . . . as a human . . . and he's been condemned to history's hell.

McClellan's greatest opponent was not Lee, nor a single Confederate. McClellan's supreme challenger was his role—his position as commander of an army—the most important army in the United States and the most visible army in the world in September, 1862. Everyone's eyes focused upon George McClellan, and he knew it.

The lasting impression of General McClellan is best summarized, perhaps, by President Lincoln's Secretary of the Navy. "McClellan is an intelligent engineer and officer, but not a commander to head a great army in the field," observed Gideon Welles. "To attack or advance with energy and power is not in him; to fight is not his forte."[90]

God graced McClellan with the fortune of Lee's Lost Order. Historians, through their annals, have branded McClellan a soldier of misfortune.

Whom should we trust?

CHAPTER 18
Charade Crescendo

[A]ffectation is fond of making
a greater show than reality.
—Lydia M. Child[91]

EXAGGERATION is a human temptation.

Everyone does it; no one avoids it. We engage in embellishment. It's our natural condition.

Historians must be alert for this omnipresent characteristic. When conducting our research—or the detective work of a historian—we must be cognizant of hyperbole and be careful not to accept it as truth. We must challenge our sources, question our discoveries and be sage with our skepticism. Discernment is our defense.

Yet some stories are just too good to resist.

Here's one. The place is Frederick. The time is just before noon on Saturday, September 13 (yes, Friday the 13th would be more dramatic). The scene—George McClellan's headquarters tent. A small group is gathered around the deliberating general. He studies something. It's Lee's Lost Order. The tense silence suddenly explodes. "Now I know what to do!" McClellan exclaims.

Powerful quotation. These few resounding words inform us—help us feel—one of the most momentous moments in American military history. Terrific theatrics; high drama. We thrive on drama. But the dispassionate historian should exercise caution and not be trapped in euphoria of emotion. Instead of a Shakespeare, when it comes to sources, we should practice like Einstein. We must be deliberate and methodical, in case something's diabolical.

The first question the discerning historian should ask actually is two: What is the source?, then who is the source?

The "Now I know what to do!" quotation was unearthed by preeminent Southern historian Douglas Southall Freeman. The original memoranda containing the quote literally arrived in Freeman's mailbox in the late 1930s—sent to him by a Confederate descendant seventy years after the Civil War.[92] Most historians, upon such a discovery, would have back flipped at this find of a lifetime. Freeman, however, relegated it to a lonely appendix, easily lost in his timeless trilogy *Lee's Lieutenants*.

The memoranda concerned the Lost Orders. The two 1868 documents summarized an interview with General Lee six years after Antietam and nearly three years after Appomattox. It claimed Lee first heard of McClellan's possession of the Lost Order through cavalry commander J.E.B. Stuart. Specifically, the memoranda stated, "Stuart learned from a gentleman of Maryland who was in McClellan's headquarters when the dispatch . . . was brought to McClellan, who after reading it, threw his hands up and exclaimed 'now I know what to do.'"[93]

Sears retold this tale in *Landscape Turned Red*, but with embellishment. The "gentleman of Maryland" became a "Confederate sympathizer." How did Sears know that? Perhaps the man—whose name is unknown—cared less about sympathies and simply had a big mouth, telling anyone who would listen what he had witnessed. Ever meet anyone like that? Sears further postulated that the mysterious man "was soon on his way through the lines, and about dusk, managed to locate Jeb Stuart near Turner's Gap [where] he explained what he had seen."[94]

Nothing in the original document transcribed by Freeman asserted this notion. Because, perhaps . . . it did not happen? Consider the difficulty, as a civilian, of barging your way through at least 3,000 U.S. infantrymen, dodging hundreds of Yankee cavalry, routing around dozens of bulky artillery, navigating through hundreds of horses and mules, following the main thoroughfare into enemy country and slipping through unnoticed? What were the odds of successfully reaching Rebel lines? Even more, what was the like-lihood of locating General Stuart, who was galloping around in-cessantly, attempting to determine what the Federals were up to? What chances of meeting with Stuart? Instead of inquisitiveness, however, historians have accepted this story as gospel.

Murfin, for his part, upstaged Sears in his version of the tale, employing more fluorescent flourish. Enjoy this irresistible pas-sage of happenstance from *The Gleam of Bayonets*:

"[McClellan] was in conference with several businessmen of Frederick, possibly discussing arrangements for supplies. One of his guests was a Southern sympathizer. It was difficult for this man to conceal his shock when McClellan threw his arms in the air and exclaimed that he now knew Lee's secret. As soon as the con-ference was completed, the man made immediate arrangements to pass through the lines. Near dusk, he approached Confederate pickets at the base of South Mountain. He had a message for Gen-eral Lee, he told the men. They took him to Jeb Stuart who . . . questioned the stranger extensively. The story the man told was utterly fantastic, but certainly one that could not be ignored. . . . Lee must be notified."[95]

Murfin acknowledged the story as "fantastic"—in other words, almost unbelievable—at that moment, in that time. But the story has turned true in historians' time, with embellishment and ex-citement galore.

The denouement of this drama revealed General Lee pulling back his forces in alarm, once alerted that McClellan had his plans. According to the original 1868 memorandu in Freeman's posses-sion, Lee reportedly said, "[I]t is probable the loss of the dispatch changed the character of the campaign."[96]

True. General Lee, for his part, made no mention of this mys-terious civilian notification in any of his 1862 writings. If so im-portant and life-altering—as historians have claimed—we would expect Lee to address it in his September 16 campaign update to President Davis. But there's nothing. Nada. In 697 words in his message to Davis, not a single word mentioned the "gentleman of Maryland"—not a peep from Lee about Stuart learning of McClel-lan's discovery of the Lost Order, and not a reference to any such fiasco. Lee, instead, acknowledged that "the enemy was advancing more rapidly than convenient." That was Lee's explanation for his unexpected withdrawal from the Pennsylvania border.[97]

Cavalry commander Stuart himself shared not a single notation of an encounter with this mysterious man in any of his contemporary reports. In his official campaign summary, comprising eight pages in the lofty Official Records of the War of the Rebellion, Stuart made no mention of meeting.[98]

Interestingly though, in General Lee's official campaign report (dated August 19, 1863—eleven months after Antietam), Lee admitted knowledge of the Lost Order: "A copy of the order directing the movement of the army from Fredericktown had fallen into the hands of General McClellan, and disclosed to him the disposition of our forces."[99]

In this matter-of-fact statement, Lee offered no details. He didn't explain when, or from whom, he learned this information. Was it, perhaps, from the "gentleman from Maryland"?

Or was George McClellan himself the source of Lee's knowledge?

How can this be? Am I accusing McClellan of providing the enemy with information, intentionally? No—though that strategy has merit. Wait . . . that makes no sense . . . unless you employ Machiavellian tactics. Leaking the orders—and permitting the Confederates to know, that you know, their intentions—is a classic Machiavellian maneuver. The result may slow Lee, stall him or even force the Rebel commander abruptly to alter his plans. From a Machiavellian perspective, perhaps the "gentleman from Maryland" (presuming he existed) was no Confederate sympathizer, but an agent on behalf of McClellan. Sound fantastic? Not any more so than the traditional and hackneyed version.

Another possible source was Yankee newspapers. General Lee received much of his intelligence concerning the Federal army and its movements through the Northern press. Censorship of military matters seldom occurred at this stage of the war, and Lee gained advantages through freedom of the press.

So enjoy this titillation. Two days after the Lost Order fell into McClellan's hands, the *Washington Star* reported the discovery on the second page of its September 15 issue. Someone had leaked to the press! The article, however, mislabeled the order as "Order No.

119." The next day, the *Baltimore Sun* published the same article verbatim.[100]

Lee typically had access to these papers. But since he was maneuvering and fighting to save his army and salvage the invasion when these papers were published, doubtless he had little time for recreational reading. Still, this could have served as the source for Lee's official report in August, 1863.

More likely McClellan's own official report informed Lee of the Lost Order. McClellan's review of the Antietam campaign was released on August 4, 1863. Published widely throughout the North, it included the verbiage of Special Orders 191 in its contents. McClellan introduced his discovery as follows: "On the 13th an order fell into my hands, issued by General Lee, which fully disclosed his plans."[101]

Compare that statement with General Lee's official campaign report, appearing only 15 days later: "A copy of the order directing the movement of the army from Fredericktown had fallen into the hands of General McClellan, and disclosed to him the disposition of our forces."[102]

Notice similarities?

CHAPTER 19

Lonely Day, Lonely Night

Our days are a kaleidoscope.
Every instant a change takes place in the contents.
New harmonies, new contrasts, new combinations of every sort.
—Henry Ward Beecher[103]

RECALL ONE OF those days.

You have everything planned. Alarm clock set; household chores completed; travel necessities in hand; pet sitter confirmed; family ready to go. Much excitement.

You arrive at the airport with ample time. Check-in completed; baggage tagged; boarding behind you and seatbelts tightened. Just like clockwork. Then . . . everything stops. You sit on the tarmac, a captive in a tubular container. For hours you are a hostage. Frustration mounts. Anger builds. Exasperated, you know you will miss the big event, as you stare frozen and powerless. Your plan has crumbled; your destination defeated. You have no control over those controlling.

How do you feel?

Now you can relate to Robert E. Lee.

There is only one constant in history—emotion. Times change, dates differ, the stage transforms. Players appear and disappear, characters alter. But the tapestry that connects all humanity, and transcends all time is our shared emotions.

General Lee had his plan. "The present seems to be the most propitious time since the commencement of the war for the Con-

federate Army to enter [the North]," assessed Lee to his president, Jefferson Davis. The U.S. armies were defeated and demoralized. New Federal recruits were not yet trained and organized. Southern sympathizing Maryland could be freed of "the oppression to which she is now subject."[104] The war would vacate Virginia and threaten Washington. Invasion would generate political instability for Lincoln and his Republicans, only weeks before mid-term elections. A show of force in the North might persuade England and France to recognize the Confederacy as a nation.

At no point since the eruption of the Civil War had Southern interests approached such climax. Lee's Confederacy was at its zenith—and near cherished independence.

To ensure optimum results, to instigate panic and chaos in enemy territory, to draw the Federal army far from D.C.'s defenses, Lee informed his president: "I propose to enter Pennsylvania."[105] Later Lee states, "I am aware that the movement [invasion] is attended with much risk, yet I do not consider success impossible."[106]

Lee, in fact, was already so near the possible. Only one week after his army marched into the North, the Confederate commander had reached Hagerstown, a scant five miles from the Mason-Dixon Line. Lee—poised to pounce into Pennsylvania—updated President Davis on September 13: "Every effort . . . will be made to acquire every advantage which our position and means may warrant."[107]

Then, an enemy earthquake struck. Collapse!

Less than twelve hours later, Lee's world had shifted dramatically. The Bluecoats were threatening South Mountain, a barrier that Lee could not allow to be breached. The Rebel dam at South Mountain, if ruptured, would expose Lee's scattered columns to danger and possible demise. If a Confederate defense of South Mountain failed, even a return to Virginia—unimaginable only hours before—now became problematic, with lines of retreat to the Potomac potentially severed. South Mountain must hold.[108]

But no Confederates were defending South Mountain. Lee ordered adjustments, repositioning his forces to contest and block the mountain's gaps. Throughout the night of the 13th and into the morning of Sunday the 14th, Lee's soldiers marched and countermarched; deployed, then redeployed, searching in the darkness for suitable positions of defense. It was a miserable night with no sleep, no food, no campfires, and of most concern, no idea what was happening.

Lee himself determined South Mountain too important to be left to subordinates. Forget Pennsylvania, for the moment. The commanding general reversed course, altering plans and abandoning Hagerstown. He relinquished, for now, his offensive. The mindset now was defensive. In the darkness, Lee wheeled the army away from Hagerstown, sending it in two directions. Most began marching toward South Mountain. Some were detained and pushed rearward toward the Potomac. Lee knew he must not lose those river crossings.

Hence the race commenced for South Mountain. The two armies collided that Sunday, with the Southerners fighting desperately to plug the mountain's gaps. They failed—or did they succeed?

Wait. Hold the narrative. This made sense until now. How can we have one battle with two different outcomes?

Welcome to History as point of view—more usual than unusual—when we consider that an elemental human trait is our choice to agree or disagree. South Mountain offers us a classic example in determinative disagreement. Who won? Who lost? Your response depends upon your point of view (and perhaps whether you were born and raised Southern or Northern . . . or just somewhere).

If you're adorned in the stars and stripes, your reaction mirrors Union commander George McClellan: "It has been a glorious victory," McClellan effused. "The information is perfectly reliable that the enemy is making for [the Potomac] in a perfect rout." The crowning achievement—"General Lee last night stated publicly that he must admit they had been shockingly whipped." Even Little Mac's chief critic, President Lincoln, concurred: "I now consider it safe to say that General McClellan has gained a great victory over the great rebel army in Maryland . . . He is now pursuing the flying foe."[109]

No room for interpretation here. This appears closed to discussion. Unless you espouse the Southern perspective. "The battle continued with great animation until night," General Lee informed his president, Jefferson Davis. "The effort to force a passage of the mountains had failed."[110]

This countered entirely McClellan's conclusion. From Lee's perspective, the Confederates had delayed the Federals; his Rebels had held them in check. Retreat routes to the river remained secure; darkness offered opportunities for adjustments. Lee had purchased an extra day—precious time—for Stonewall Jackson to complete his Harpers Ferry mission.

These achievements, however, could belie reality. Too many Federals threatened the crest of South Mountain. Lee knew he was outnumbered. He realized his flanks were endangered. Intelligence informed him more enemy was en route. Lee assessed these negatives, understood dire consequences awaited on the morrow,

and drew one conclusion: "I feared [we] would be unable to renew the fight in the morning."[111]

Never before had Robert E. Lee ordered a retreat. Never before had his army suffered defeat. In 24 hours, Lee had gone from threatening Pennsylvania to threatened nearly out of existence. Never had a single day created so much disarray.

Lee stared objectively at his situation. Then he wrote the most distressing words of his career.

"The day has gone against us and this army will go by Sharpsburg and cross the river."[112]

Invasion . . . canceled.

CHAPTER 20
Through God's Blessing

It irritates me to be told how things have always been done.
I defy the tyranny of precedent.
I cannot afford the luxury of a closed mind.
—Clara Barton[113]

SOMEONE ONCE MUSED that Stonewall Jackson avoided a fight on Sundays.

The deeply religious Presbyterian general, according to the musing, desired to avoid battle on the Sabbath to honor God's day of rest.

Quite a fable. Jackson earned his sobriquet Stonewall on a July Sunday while standing firm on Henry Hill in the first major battle of the Civil War at First Manassas. Eight months later on a Sunday in March, Jackson was thrashed in his only defeat of the war when his men abandoned a stone wall in the Shenandoah Valley Battle of Kernstown. On the last Sunday of May, two months later, Jackson redeemed his lone loss, forcing the Yankees into an embarrassing retreat at the Battle of First Winchester. Two weeks later, on the second Sunday in June, Stonewall defended rolling hills at Cross Keys in the heart of the Shenandoah Valley. The Lord's Day, overall, had been a day for Stonewall Jackson to fight.

Sunday, September 14th, heralded another Stonewall Sunday. This one, however, could prove dreadfully dire.

Jackson's patience had reached its limits. The Union defenders at Harpers Ferry had resisted. Surrounded they were, but surrendered they had not. Worse still (but unbeknown to Jackson), garrison commander Dixon Miles had dispatched a courier to General McClellan, delivering Miles's plea for prompt reinforcement, hoping he could hold on for forty-eight hours. The stubborn Federals showed no signs of submission. Making matters more miserable, Stonewall knew he was late—now two days behind schedule in completing his Special Orders 191 assignment. Exasperated and confounded, Jackson had had enough.

The moment required measures that were, by standards of that day, brutally extreme.

"So soon as you get your batteries all planted, let me know," Old Jack dispatched to his subordinate commander holding Maryland Heights. "I desire . . . to send in a flag of truce, for the purpose of getting out the noncombatants [living in Harpers Ferry], should the commanding officer refuse to surrender."

Then Jackson's message turned ominous. "Should we have to attack, let the work be done thoroughly; fire on the houses when necessary. The citizens can keep out of harm's way from your artillery. Demolish the place if it is occupied by the enemy, and does not surrender."[114]

Oh my. Never in American history had American cannon been turned upon American citizens. More troublesome, Harpers Ferry lay within the Confederate nation. These were homes of fellow Virginians. Men from Harpers Ferry served within Jackson's ranks. Women and children and old men (the noncombatants) could be killed or maimed or suddenly homeless. What did this mean? And on a Sunday?

Jackson had no time for moral philosophy. But time itself was burdening Stonewall. Noon passed, and still the Confederates were dragging guns up the indomitable inclines of Maryland and Loudoun Heights. No artillery assignment (and perhaps none other during the entire Civil War) had been this difficult. Mother Nature herself was conducting combat against Jackson.

Complicating matters, Jackson undoubtedly knew that the Federal Army was coming. General Lee had dispatched communiqués to warn him. But if even had their delivery failed, Jackson probably heard Union cannon booming to announce the Yankee advance. It was probable he heard rumbles from the artillery blasting into the gaps of South Mountain. McClellan's men were maneuvering to catch Jackson's Confederates "in their own trap."

Further frustrating Jackson, he could not employ his infamous infantry. "The position in front of me [Bolivar Heights] is a strong one," Stonewall grumbled. He realized a frontal assault, across one mile of open ground, was problematic. Worse still, once at the base of Bolivar, the mountain soared 300 vertical feet, just like a castle wall. Never had Stonewall faced such a substantive enemy fortress, buttressed by nearly 11,000 U.S. infantrymen and nearly 60 cannon upon the crest of Bolivar Heights. Jackson recognized it—any direct stab at Bolivar Heights was suicidal. He must control his aggressive instincts. "I desire to remain quiet," he demurred. Now Stonewall's artillery must pummel the Yankees into submission.[115]

Jackson's gunners pounded the hapless Federals for four hours that Sunday afternoon. "At first their missiles of death fell far short of our camp," recalled a raw-recruit lieutenant from New York. "[B]ut each succeeding shell came nearer and nearer, until the earth was plowed up at our feet, and our tents torn to tatters."[116]

But the tactic failed. As darkness draped the Harpers Ferry valley, no white flags appeared. Miles remained tenacious.

Flustered and flummoxed, Old Jack was growing desperate. He had to attempt the unconventional—night assault! . . . or at least the ruse of an attack in the darkness.

Seldom during the Civil War did fighting occur at night. No one could see. The tactics of the time required long parallel lines, sometimes nearly 1,000 yards wide, advancing in tandem toward a target, supported by long-range artillery firing overhead. Consider the chaos of maintaining formation (not to mention your own cannoneers not knowing your whereabouts) caused by darkness. But one certainly could generate a noisy and impressive demonstration, and scare the enemy into belief.

Jackson launched his fake attack against Bolivar Heights on Sunday night about 8 p.m. The ruse worked. Colonel Miles pulled troops from other sectors to defend, opening a hole on his left flank, through which Stonewall secretly penetrated with thousands of stealth infantry and 20 cannon.[117]

Sunrise the next morning unveiled the Confederate mischief. The U.S. position was untenable, and every Yankee knew it. At close range, the Rebels opened a battering barrage. "The infernal screech owls came hissing and singing," recorded a frightened Federal, "then bursting, plowing great holes in the earth, filling our eyes with dust, and tearing many giant trees to atoms." Another captured the moment: "A general feeling of depression observable in all the men. . . . All seem to think that we will have to surrender or be cut to pieces."[118]

Colonel Miles and his officers concurred. White flags (actually dozens of white handkerchiefs attached to artillery implements, sword blades, flag stanchions and musket barrels) began showing about 8 a.m.

"Through God's blessing," a grateful Jackson penned in his victory note to General Lee, "Harpers Ferry and its garrison are to be surrendered."[119]

Then off galloped a courier in search of the commanding general.

CHAPTER 21
Fight or Flight

There are in this world two kinds of nature—
those that have wings, and those that have feet . . .
The walking are the logicians;
The winged are the instinctive and poetic.
—Harriett Beecher Stowe[120]

YOU KNOW THE FEELING.

Trouble consumes you. You're trembling in tremendous trouble. Or danger. You're shaking in serious danger. What do you do? Stand your ground and defend yourself? Or seek an escape and flee post haste?

Every animal on the planet possesses the instinct of fight or flight. It's triggered by our will to survive. The degrees of our experiences differ, but every human at some point faces this awful dilemma.

My first understanding of this fundamental physiologic response occurred when I was in high school. Halloween had arrived, and the seniors were responsible for "fright night" at my church. In addition to the usual scare tactics, we decided to have a body rise from the grave (appropriate for church, we reasoned). I volunteered as the body. My peers stuffed me into a makeshift wooden box, placed me in a freshly excavated hole in the ground, and slammed the lid. So far, so good. But then a prankster began shoveling dirt onto the box. . . .

My metaphoric experience (pardon me) illustrates the predicament of General Lafayette McLaws. The burly Georgian with thick curly hair and a wavy black beard shared the cranial features of Jerry Garcia on stage with the Grateful Dead. As you cogitate on that image, consider McLaws' serious assignment in Special Orders 191, specifically: 1) advance upon Harpers Ferry from the north; 2) seize Maryland Heights, the highest mountain looming over the Ferry; 3) coordinate with Stonewall Jackson on the envelopment of the U.S. garrison; and 4) reunite with the army when mission completed.[121]

McLaws completed tasks one through three promptly, including victory in a day-long battle to gain control of Maryland Heights. Task No. 4, however, had mutated into a serious problem.

Due to unexpected Federal resistance and the Unionists' refusal to surrender at the Ferry, coupled with a rescue mission ordered there by General McClellan, McLaws had become trapped—literally sealed in a six-mile box. Two mountain ranges compressed his sides, with his toes squashed by the Yankees at Harpers Ferry and his head squeezed by Bluecoats who had penetrated South Mountain at Crampton's Gap. For McLaws, it was too late for flight; his only recourse was fight.

General Lee, twenty-five miles distant at Hagerstown, had perceived this peril on the night of September 13. Alerted to the startling advances of the Northerners, Lee warned McLaws: "You are particularly desired to watch well the main road from Frederick to Harpers Ferry, so as to prevent the enemy from turning your position." Lee then promulgated this desire: "The commanding general hopes that the enemy about Harpers Ferry will be speedily disposed of."[122] But neither Lee nor McLaws controlled the Ferry clock; and now McLaws was boxed-in and stuck.

Lee pleaded for him to escape on Sunday night, the 14th. "It is necessary for you to abandon your position tonight."[123] Relying on his familiarity with the region from leading John Brown's capture three years earlier, Lee recommended one outlet—a break in the box at Solomon's Gap in the Elk Ridge (the mountain sealing McLaws from the left side). So anxious was General Lee to salvage McLaws, he halted the retreat of his army from South Mountain, stopping near Sharpsburg, "with a view of preventing the enemy from cutting you off, and enabling you to make a junction with [me]."[124]

This appeared doable on a map, but McLaws dismissed the vent at Solomon's Gap as impractical. Moving 8,000 soldiers through a boulder-strewn pass via a narrow and unfamiliar road in the darkness seemed impossible. "[C]ould not pass over mountain except in a scattered and disorganized condition," McLaws determined. "In no contingency could I have saved the trains and artillery."[125]

So McLaws disobeyed direct orders from his army commander, General Lee. How does that typically end?

The consequences must wait, as he summed up his top priority: "I had nothing to do but to defend my position."[126]

Surmising he was outnumbered (he was, three to two), McLaws, beaver-like, worked all night to erect a dam of Confederate soldiers across Pleasant Valley. In the darkness he positioned two parallel lines of Graycoats, each stretching nearly one mile from the base of South Mountain to the pedestal of Elk Ridge. Every soldier from every sector was moved into line, with artillery aligned in support.

This operation required the removal of men from Maryland Heights. What had been McLaws' front now became his rear. McLaws drew no fear from the Harpers Ferry quarter, as the Potomac acted like a moat. Indeed, a pontoon bridge crossed the moat, but surely the Federals would not cross the moat that night.

Bad assumption. As General McLaws was preparing for a fight, Dixon Miles ordered a flight. Simultaneous with McLaws' abandonment of Maryland Heights, the U.S. commander at Harpers Ferry—who knew nothing of the Confederate redeployment—was gambling he could sneak under the nose of the Maryland mountain. Miles had nearly 1,400 cavalry at his disposal—useless in a siege operation (for lovers of equines, I apologize for labeling your pets useless). What if they could break out? The previous night (the 13th), Miles had attempted a similar tactic, but on a very small scale. He launched a tiny detachment in a desperate attempt "to reach somebody that had ever heard of the United States Army, or any general of the United States Army, or anybody that knew anything about the United States Army, and report the condition of Harpers Ferry."[127] Miraculously, this mission succeeded, reporting to McClellan on the 14th.

But Miles didn't know it. Assuming failure, in a Hail Mary, Miles instructed his remaining cavalry to cross the pontoon, turn left under the nose of Maryland Heights, and head northward to Sharpsburg. Surely, somewhere in the North, the cavalry would find Northerners.

Instead, it located Southerners—upon the thousands. First at Sharpsburg, where it encountered Lee's retreating army. With that route blocked, it diverted toward Williamsport, where it astonishingly discovered gold!—a lightly guarded Rebel munitions train. The Yankees promptly captured the prize and then escorted their spoils into Pennsylvania.[128] Though heralded as a great exploit (100 percent happenstance, of course), this escapade did nothing to save Colonel Miles. Nor did Miles realize that it had revealed a gaping hole in the Confederate noose strangling Harpers Ferry. Had Miles known that the Rebels had departed Maryland Heights, could the rest of his men have escaped too?

Meanwhile, as the sun rose on the morning of the 15th, there stood Lafayette McLaws, five miles north of Harpers Ferry—isolated, alone and staring into the throat of disaster. But then a strange occurrence. "[T]he enemy did not advance," reported an astonished McLaws. More peculiar, "nor did they offer any opposition to the troops taking position across the valley."[129]

What was happening?

Mirage.

"They outnumber me two to one," dispatched the nervous Federal commander facing McLaws. "I shall wait here until I learn the prospect of re-enforcement."[130]

Neither fight nor flight saved General McLaws.

Fear (by his opponent) offered him salvation.

CHAPTER 22

Scapegoat

No man for any considerable period
can wear one face to himself and another to the multitude,
without finally getting bewildered
as to which may be true.
—Nathaniel Hawthorne[131]

HAVE YOU EVER BEEN BLAMED for something, when you believe you didn't deserve it? Well, then, you'd make an ideal character in history.

Historians enjoy assigning blame. Someone must be at fault for failure. And once consigned, it's an indelible tattoo that becomes nearly impossible to escape.

Bringing to mind the scapegoat. We know its meaning—a branding we never desire—but what of its origin?

The Bible, interestingly, is the source of the scapegoat. In Leviticus 16:8, we discover one goat is selected to carry away the sins of the community and cast them into the desert (we can presume humans opted for the goat, not God). The creature has not the ill-repute of the snake, but the goat's agility in climbing mountains and descending valleys ensured sins would be carried as far away as possible. So, the original scapegoat is a compliment to the animal's abilities. When people apply the term to people, the person's (and the goat's) reputation is damaged irreparably.

Fascinating, as Mr. Spock would say. No. 191—that's the total number of words in the paragraphs above (for those who are anal, that includes the chapter heading, title and introductory quotation). Quite a coincidence. Special Orders 191 certainly produced its share of scapegoats, as blame was doled out on all sides. General Lee for overestimating the prowess of his men and underestimating the moves of McClellan. Stonewall Jackson for tardiness and failure to acknowledge enemy resistance. General McClellan for . . . well, everything . . . according to most historians. And poor Colonel Miles at Harpers Ferry for not defending the most defensible Maryland Heights. And there's a slew more to come (remember we historians excel at scapegoating).

Now I'd like to introduce you to the superior supine scapegoat—superior because there's no one more fitting to wear the mantel than Union General William B. Franklin, who defines the word supine (I'll save you the trouble—utterly passive or inactive).

William Buel Franklin was a 39-year old debonair chap with a pedigree in politics. His father served as clerk of the U.S. House of Representatives during his teenage days, and his great grandfather was a member of the First Continental Congress. A native of Pennsylvania, he attended West Point, graduating first in his class. The army employed its smartest people as civil engineers (the bottom of the class was exiled into the infantry); and Franklin commenced building forts and bridges and railroads and—the U.S. Capitol dome. When the war erupted, he became an ally of McClellan's and an enemy of the anti-slavery Republicans.

Now his friend McClellan called upon him to inflict damage upon the real enemy—Lee's Confederates.

Since the Rebel invasion had commenced, Franklin's force of nearly 12,000 men had been crawling along the Potomac since departing Washington. McClellan devised this strategy to ensure the Confederates did not exploit a defensive loophole and suddenly dash along the river toward the capital. So as the rest of the U.S. army swung north and west toward Frederick in pursuit of Lee, Franklin served as the hinge on the door, more in a posture of defense.

That stratagem ended suddenly with the discovery of Special Orders 191.

"I have now full information as to the movements and intentions of the enemy," McClellan informed Franklin in a 6:20 p.m.

General William B. Franklin.
Courtesy of the Library of Congress.

dispatch on September 13. He then ordered his subordinate to commence marching toward beleaguered Harpers Ferry, but not until at dawn on the 14th—a delay that has buried McClellan under volcanic eruptions of critical historians. Once started, McClellan made clear Franklin's mission, which was "to cut off, destroy, or capture McLaws' command and relieve Colonel Miles." McClellan did not undersell the mission's importance: "I ask of you, at this important moment, all your intellect and the utmost activity that a general can exercise."[132]

This order, upon first reading, appears conflicted and counter-intuitive. Your mission is urgent, says McClellan, but don't move yet. What's the deal?

Historians' myopic and microscopic focus upon eighteen hours—from the time McClellan received the Lost Order about noon on the 13th until Franklin moved at dawn on the 14th—has dominated the debate. As explained in Chapter 16, it's also among the things that have been mischaracterized and misrepresented to demonize Little Mac.

But this intentional delay can be explained. No, I'm not defending or protecting McClellan. That very thought makes me queasy. But I must demur. As American educator Amos Bronson Alcott said, "A true teacher defends his pupils against his own personal influences."[133]

McClellan envisioned a strategy greater than a direct stab at Harpers Ferry. Based upon information within the Lost Order, Lee's instructions specified the exact location of every division in the Rebel army. This informed McClellan, that two divisions under General McLaws were north of Harpers Ferry. This comprised the greatest concentration of Confederate strength blocking (potentially) the southern gaps at South Mountain leading to Harpers Ferry. Franklin, therefore, would be encountering the enemy alone.[134]

This presented risk, in McClellan's mind. Franklin's force was by itself—detached, alone. So to render assistance, McClellan planned a right hook. He would bust his main army through South Mountain at Turner's Gap, seven miles north of Franklin. Then swiftly swing south and hammer the Rebels on their flank, as Franklin shadow boxed on their front. McClellan was specific: "If you find the pass [in front of you] held by the enemy in large force, make all your dispositions for attack, and commence it about half an hour after you hear severe firing at the pass [seven miles north] . . . where the main body will attack."[135]

Franklin followed this instruction to the letter. Too bad.

Here's where he deserved blame. When he arrived at the base of Crampton's Gap, no "large force" opposed him. He outnumbered a thin line of Rebel defenders thirteen to one. These are good odds. Even if you're not a gambler, you'll win 93 percent of the time.

But here surfaced two fatal flaws that doomed Franklin to inaction—First was "McClellanitis," an infectious disease that tricked the mind into doubling or tripling enemy numbers; and second, his career as an engineer.

Engineers, by design, adhere to instructions. Precise. Methodical. Calculating. Checking the formula and testing the instruments over and again. We want engineers to build bridges. We want engineers to design our vehicles. We want engineers constructing skyscrapers. With this mindset—plodding precision and precision to perfection—do you want an engineer leading an army?

These two character traits conspired to freeze Franklin at the foot of Crampton's Gap. Blinded from recognizing the obvious (minimal resistance), Franklin wasted six hours (facing light opposition) before attaining the crest of the mountain. He was not the right man, at the right place, to exercise independent thought while leading an independent command. The condemnation, here, for unwarranted delay, is deserved.

Doubly deserved the next day, September 15. A severe bout of "McClellanitis" seized Franklin early that morning, as he gazed down upon two parallel lines of McLaws' Rebels stretching across Pleasant Valley before him. For a man ordered to utilize "all your intellect and the utmost activity that a general can exercise," to rescue Harpers Ferry, the engineer Franklin responded:

"They outnumber me two to one."[136]

First at West Point, indeed.

A bad calculator, however, on the battlefield.

CHAPTER 23
Four-Letter Words

Progress is the victory of a new thought
over old superstitions.
—Elizabeth Cady Stanton[137]

PEOPLE OF THE VICTORIAN ERA impress us.

Prim with their mannerisms. Proper with their rules of etiquette. Polite in their relationships. Pure in their intentions. This, at least, is what their literature tells us.

No people are like that. Queen Victoria and her noble English court, perhaps (though we now know that none of them were pure). But they don't reflect the commoner, the typical farm boy, the recent immigrant, the street merchant, the coal miner, the train conductor, the iron-mill worker, the canal-boat operator and the plethora of professions that determined the destiny of the democratic republic of America.

Even our elected leaders made a unique impression. The celebrated British novelist Charles Dickens decided to visit our peculiar land twenty years before the Civil War, and his inspection of our Capitol—our seat of government—left an impression disparate from English court. "Both houses are handsomely carpeted," observed Dickens, "but the state to which these carpets are reduced by the universal disregard of the spittoon . . . and the extraordinary improvements on the pattern which are squirted and dabbled upon it in every direction, do not admit of being described." Upon further reflection, Dickens continued. "I strongly recommend all strangers not to look at the floor; and if they happen to drop anything, though it be their purse, not to pick it up."

Dickens also discovered our legislators a breed of their own, sporting "swelled faces" caused by "the quantity of tobacco they contrive to stow within the hollow of the cheek." The English novelist concluded that a congressman was too surreal even for one of his novels. "It is strange enough, too, to see an honorable gentleman leaning back in his tilted chair, with his legs on the desk before him, shaping a convenient 'plug' with his penknife, and when it is quite ready for use, shooting the old one from his mouth as from a pop-gun, and clapping the new one in its place."[138]

Dickens never met Robert E. Lee, but if he had, he would have discovered his "English gentry" in America. History often has characterized Lee as "the last cavalier"—a man of dignity and deportment and distinction, quite the antithesis of the roughneck rabble Dickens encountered and described. Lee defined a "FFV" (First Family of Virginia), a distinction of nobility not earned, but birthed. His father, "Light Horse Harry" Lee, gained fame as a cavalry officer in George Washington's Revolutionary army; he knew Washington so well that he authored the words "first in war, first in peace, and first in the hearts of his countrymen." Robert himself continued the Washington association, marrying into the family and inheriting Arlington plantation, including the famed colonnaded mansion overlooking the U.S. capital.

Wealthy and secure and a slave owner, Lee rebuffed the planter's lifestyle in exchange for the austerity and uncertain life of a professional soldier. Following his graduation from West Point (second in his class, and with no demerits), Lee spent the next 31 years serving in the United States Army, including a stint as West Point superintendent.

Lee watched the onslaught of secession with foreboding. "As far as I can judge by the papers, we are between a state of anarchy and civil war," he wrote his wife three months before war erupted. "As an American citizen, I take great pride in my country, her prosperity and institutions ... but I can anticipate no greater calamity for the country than a dissolution," he shared with his son Custis.

To a friend he conjectured: "God alone can save us from our folly, selfishness and short sightedness. . . . I only see that a fearful calamity is upon us, and fear that the country will have to pass through for its sins a fiery ordeal."[139]

Less than two years later (September 1862), Lee was commanding an army opposing the United States, defeating United States armies and poised to launch an invasion into the United States. Never before had Lee come so near achieving independence for his new nation—the Confederate States of America.

But that vision appeared on the verge of collapse. Lee now wandered in the darkness of Western Maryland, his army in full retreat. Nothing had turned out well for Marse Robert in the past 36 hours. Surprised by the unexpected aggressive advances of the foe; compelled to withdraw the invasion force from the Pennsylvania line; forced to fight an undesired battle to save his scattered army; required to retreat for the first time as an army commander; and suffering from the pain of defeat, Lee was witness to victory vanishing.

The general no doubt pondered these burdens during the long, aggravating, miserable night of September 14-15. Worst of all, he had cancelled the invasion. The operation had turned so badly, he had no choice. He now was within three miles of Virginia, near a hamlet called Sharpsburg, along the Antietam Creek. It was best to return home, reunite the army, and plan for the next campaign.

Then a horse's gallop broke through the heavy night air. A courier arrived with a message—a note from Stonewall Jackson at Harpers Ferry: "Through God's blessing, the advance, which commenced this evening, has been successful so far." Lee certainly straightened, as his eyes peered through his glasses, studying the dispatch in the dim candlelight. Good news—the first good news in nearly two days. Jackson continued: "I look to Him [God] for complete success tomorrow."[140]

Lee sensed confidence from Jackson. No equivocation. No problems. No more delays. Harpers Ferry would fall, and soon.

At that moment—at that instant—we don't know the thoughts of Robert E. Lee.

But we do know his actions.

I describe this, and term this, as "Lee's Four-Letter Words."

First is *Rest*. Let the men rest. Lee's force (about one-third of the army accompanying him) had been in motion for the past twenty-four hours. No food. No sleep. A battle as well, and now a midnight retreat. Lee reasoned he could concentrate his troops on the west bank of the Antietam, where the creek itself would serve as a temporary Maginot Line and ward off any pursuers. No Federals were pursuing that night, but Lee did not know that. The Antietam offered a barrier—and an opportunity for rest.

Wait is the second word. Wait for Jackson to finish his mission at Harpers Ferry and then await Stonewall's arrival. Two of every three soldiers in Lee's army were not with Lee, but with Jackson. The investment of Harpers Ferry had detained most of the Confederates. The distance between Lee and Jackson, via the most direct Virginia route and Boteler's Ford across the Potomac, was about 13 miles—a one day march. Simply wait for Stonewall's "Foot Cavalry."

Join is Word No. 3. For the first time in five days, since the army divided at Frederick and scattered into four parts to execute Special Orders 191, Lee could reunite, march together and most important, fight together. Lee didn't know the strength of his opponent, but he realized he was outnumbered and, as always, overmatched by the military muscle of the U.S.

The biggest question, perhaps, was not when to join the fight, but where? Should the army's unification occur while still in Maryland? Or should Lee retire across the Potomac, and unite in the friendly confines of home (Virginia), with the river a barrier between himself and a pursuing enemy? This second option, certainly, was the safest.

Lee selected option one—remain in Maryland. Though more fraught with peril, the Gray Fox had entered Maryland with expectations. None had been realized. Other than the pending capture of Harpers Ferry, Lee had no results. The retreat from South Mountain, in fact, had been a setback. By staying in Maryland, and waiting for Jackson to join him at Sharpsburg, Lee could reconstitute the invasion.

This significant decision leads to our next word—*Move*. Move the army once Jackson arrives.

Hold on. Wait. You're addling my brains. If General Lee moves away from Sharpsburg, there's no Battle of Antietam.

Correct. But you're wise to September 17. You know what happens, because you're a time-traveler from the present into the past. My chronology, however, is two days earlier. My calendar day is Monday the 15th, and General Lee is with me. So, set your time-travel machine for September 15, and stop projecting into the future.

Let's return to *move*. Pennsylvania was near. The border and the Mason-Dixon Line are only 15 miles north of Sharpsburg. Just one day's march. Invasion of Pennsylvania, from the outset, had been the principal goal. The way was open, the road was good. Why make a stand at Sharpsburg with the real prize of Pennsylvania so near at hand? Invasion on—again!

As Lee mulled his options that damp September night, no doubt these four-letter words kept dancing around his fertile mind. But there was one more word.

Risk. What dangers lurked if Lee decided to rest? What hazards menaced if Lee determined to wait? What threats jeopardized the army if Lee elected to join at Sharpsburg? What perils awaited Lee if he resolved to move?

Lee understood risk. He had earned his reputation through risk. Risk did not frighten, but emboldened, R. E. Lee.

But there's an inherent problem with risk, and Lee knew that too.

You cannot predict the outcome.

CHAPTER 24

Linus's Blanket

*The simplest truths often meet the sternest resistance
and are slow in getting general acceptance.*
—Frederick Douglass[141]

WE LOVE LINUS.

Charles Schultz's adorable cartoon character often steals the show. We see him in the Christmas scene, on stage in a soliloquy, citing the story of Jesus's birth. And we sit with him for hours in the frosty Halloween patch awaiting the arrival of the Great Pumpkin. Soft-spoken, occasionally brilliant, and often an intellect, Linus makes the perfect foil for his brash, big-mouthed, boisterous big sister and her bullying.

But Linus has a crutch. Never do we see him without his dependency—his comfort, his courage—his blanket.

The blanket, of course, is Linus's protector. He fights like a monster to keep it; he shrivels and shakes without it. It's his cover. It keeps him safe and warm, but also serves as his defensive shield. He also can hide behind it, when necessary, if life becomes just too tough. We all relate to Linus's blanket, as we each have our own.

George McClellan wrapped himself within his own Linus blanket—exaggerated enemy numbers.

Oh, wait. Hit pause. There's that number 191 again. My word processor keeps flashing the numeral as it counts words. This time it landed upon "numbers" from the previous paragraph, as if

121

Allan Pinkerton, beside President Lincoln, in photo taken south of
Sharpsburg at the Showman Farm (aka Home Farm),
McClellan's headquarters, on October 3, 1862.
Courtesy of the Library of Congress.

adding extra emphasis to the importance of numbers, in relation
to the Lost Order.

Pardon my brief fascination with this weird pattern.

We now return to General McClellan, who was fixated on and
infected by Confederate troop strengths. Since first appointed
general-in-chief early in the war, McClellan had grappled with the
number of Southern men filling the Rebel ranks. This made good
sense. Generals throughout history have sought information on
the size and strength of their opponents.

One could not make reasoned judgments with irrational and
insufficient data. Hence, somewhere in the annals of war, we had
the birth of military intelligence. Military intelligence, hmmm.
Isn't that the definition of an oxymoron?

Regardless of wild guesses, hyperbolized hypotheses, and frequent errors, the military depends upon gathering intelligence. So did George McClellan.

Intelligence assemblage is an imperfect science. Sometimes it strikes its mark (Eisenhower prior to D-Day) and sometimes it's in the twilight zone (Saddam Hussein and weapons of mass destruction). To help determine information about Confederates, George McClellan hired a detective—Allan Pinkerton.

Pinkerton had a storied career as a detective long before the Civil War. A Scotsman who immigrated to America about twenty years before the war, he settled in Illinois and became Chicago's first police detective. He first encountered McClellan while chasing train robbers in the Midwest, and he gained fame for uncovering an assassination plot against President-elect Lincoln, as he was en route to his first inauguration.

Pinkerton employed traditional means to garner Confederate intelligence: imbedded spies, local Union loyalists, prisoners of war, enslaved populations, and Southern newspapers all provided information. But Pinkerton utilized some sort of mysterious calculator that consistently inflated Rebel troop strengths. His formulas typically doubled, and on occasion tripled, enemy strength. Lincoln and his Secretary of War considered Pinkerton's numbers bogus and ludicrous. But McClellan gave them credence.

No one in the United States knew General Lee's numbers when he invaded the North. For that matter, General Lee didn't know. As his army crossed the Potomac, with perhaps half of his men without shoes, Lee suffered from straggling of worrisome proportions. His pace was too rapid and the marches too long for men who suffered from illnesses to keep up. They also lacked clothing and shoes, as well as good food. "One great embarrassment is the reduction of our ranks by straggling," Lee apprised President Davis nine days after entering Maryland. "[I]t seems impossible to prevent . . . Our ranks are very much diminished—I fear from a third to one-half of the original numbers."[142]

Based upon Pinkerton's additions, and Lee's equal subtractions, McClellan should have expected a balanced fight.

But McClellan suffered from his own self-created and self-injected disease—"McClellanitis" (my clinical term)—the propensity to exaggerate Confederate troop strength.

"All the evidence that has been accumulated from various sources . . . goes to prove most conclusively that almost the entire [R]ebel army . . . not less than 120,000 men, is in the vicinity of Frederick City."[143]

Lee could only wish. All Confederate armies combined, fighting around Richmond when the summer of 1862 commenced, did total about 112,000 soldiers. But let's do some math (Caution! Historians are terrible at mathematics):

112,000
- 36,000 (casualties from 11 battles from June 29—Sept. 2)
- 13,000 (retained in the Richmond environs for defense)[144]
= 63,000

So, as you can see, McClellan's number of 120,000 Confederates at Frederick is quite precise—almost exactly double.

In fairness to McClellan, he did not suffer "McClellanitis" alone. The disease was actually quite contagious. Northern newspapers presented wildly varying numbers; but we know not to believe "fake news." McClellan's cavalry chief, obtaining information from the field, vacillated between 40,000 to nearly triple that number. McClellan's boss, Henry Halleck, informed the Secretary of Treasury: "From the best evidence I have—not satisfactory, but the best—I reckon the whole number . . . at 150,000." The governor of Pennsylvania, according to his sources, wired Washington with a figure of 200,000.[145]

As credit to McClellan's faith in God, one report came from a Maryland clergyman who, "a reliable man," placed the count at 120,000. That Higher Confirmation was enough for Little Mac.[146]

Regardless of numbers roulette, McClellan always claimed inferior forces. To make up for his deficit (supposed), he would politely beg, and if that didn't work yell and holler, for reinforcements. "The momentous consequences involved in the struggle of the next few days," he informed Halleck, "impels me, at the risk of being considered slow and overcautious, to most earnestly recommend that every available man be at once added to this army."

That was the polite beg. Now here was the holler—with associated threat: "[T]he result of a general battle, with such odds as the enemy now appears to have against us, might, to say the least, be doubtful; and if we should be defeated the consequences to the country would be disastrous in the extreme."[147]

This was classic McClellan. Give me what I demand; otherwise, the consequences belong to you. I admit, my own "despicable" thermometer is rising.

Three months before, in a similar note to Secretary of War Edwin Stanton sent while engaged in battle about Richmond, Little Mac howled: "I regret my great inferiority in numbers, but feel that I am in no way responsible . . . if [my army] is destroyed by overwhelming numbers, [I] can at least die with it and share its fate [editor's note: martyrdom]. But if the result of the action . . . is a disaster, the responsibility cannot be thrown on my shoulders; it must rest where it belongs."[148] (editor's note: don't blame me).

His antics prompted this response from the Secretary of War: "If he had a million men, he would swear the enemy had two millions, and then he would sit down in the mud and yell for three."[149]

Perhaps the quintessential observation on McClellan's penchant for puffery came from historian T. Harry Williams, writing near the time of the Civil War Centennial: "This inability to see things as they were," Williams perceived, "is the key to the whole McClellan problem. He saw everything as he wanted it to be. Almost literally he lived in a world of make-believe."[150]

But I offer a counter-argument to Williams. What if McClellan did believe these numbers?

Historians discredit McClellan as a fool—fooled by his own self-delusion. But historians have the luxury of looking backward. We know the Confederate numbers are bogus, but we've had 150 years to discover them, discern them, and study them.

McClellan had no such advantage. Lee was not providing him with his monthly returns (a principal source of numbers used by historians today). McClellan depended upon sources available to him, at the moment at that time.

General McClellan is not the first or last to receive bad information. Consider how often our own intelligence is suspect today, using modern satellites that can read a license plate while circling miles above earth; with wire tapping; with sophisticated GPS tracking; and with magnified scopes that can see for miles, even at night. Yes, we can collect more data; but that doesn't mean we interpret it better.

And here's a thought. What if McClellan knew the numbers were contrived? What if he realized they were inflated and deliberately bogus? What could McClellan gain by espousing—even grousing over—fantasy numbers?

Protection. Dual protection.

Let's assume McClellan was employing Machiavellian tactics to promote and promulgate Confederate strengths. An ideal framing—he would never be the loser.

As the underdog, for example, McClellan would spurn superior numbers, win the titanic struggle, and stand upon the pedestal as a mythical hero—the "Young Napoleon," as he fashioned himself.

If, however, McClellan faced an enemy double his strength, and he was whipped—the disaster was expected; the outcome predicted; the circumstances beyond his control. It was not his fault.

Brilliant.

Perhaps McClellan, to protect himself, draped himself in his own Linus Blanket.

CHAPTER 25

Secret Line

Yet the deepest truths are best read between the lines,
and, for the most part, refuse to be written.
—Bronson Alcott[151]

WOULD YOU LIKE TO HEAR a secret?

Oh, so many times have we been titillated by those seven magic words.

Our eyes flash, our eyebrows raise, our lips curl and start to smirk, our pulse begins racing as we lean in to hear whispers of wonder. Then suddenly, through a passage of souls, you're on the inside. You know something that's supposed to be unknown. You're part of a special bond of trust. The thrill!

Then comes the hard part—don't tell anyone.

We all have secrets. Each of us creates our own secrets every day—something only we know about ourselves. The fact that human beings are an elevated species (according to us), and that evolution developed us as communicators (we talk too much), has doomed the definitional meaning of secret. It's nearly impossible for us to keep something to ourselves.

Want to know my secret?

It's my favorite. This secret yields me power. It makes people ogle at me (even google me) in their amazement. It's not in my public speaking, a skill that shivers the spines of most Americans, the country's number one phobia (more so than encounters with rattlesnakes and spiders and politicians). Nor is the secret within this writing, a work now deemed excessive because I did not complete this book in 140 characters.

The secret that permits me to mesmerize audiences is the secret of the battlefield—the line.

Incoming!

My fellow Civil War historians are hurling shot and shell at me. They are indignant. For years they've trusted me never to reveal the secret. For my entire career I've carried the burden of keeping the secret within the miniscule fraternal order of Civil War scholars. I've been warned of dire consequences if I dared decode the secret. Well, my brethren, you've been defrocked.

It's all about "the line." Everything you need to know about a Civil War battle revolves around "the line." If you understand "the line," all else makes sense. No more confusion, no more disorientation, no more stupors of stupidity. Once you apply the principle of "the line," every Civil War battlefield can be comprehended— easily.

I'm certain I'll be disbarred. But finally, after half a century of secreting the secret, my soul is free from the power I've wielded on the battlefields.

The line—every Civil War battle, whether a few hours, a day, days or even months—is all about the line. Civil War tactics required soldiers to align in lines, march in lines, fight in lines and die in lines. If you lost your line, you literally were lost. Men arranged themselves, when forming the line, in such tight formation that their elbows literally touched the elbows of men to their right and left. Civil War infantry was taught and trained never to lose contact with elbows. This maintained a human chain—sometimes stretching a thousand yards in length—moving collectively, stepping in sync, glued all together into one gargantuan line.

There were two types of lines: One, the offensive line and two, the defensive line. Sorry to inform you that American football did not invent this terminology. But the line principle we watch in the game of football is no different from Civil War tactics. The offense attacks; the defense holds. Every Civil War battle was about the tactics of a line moving forward (offense) in an attempt to break through the line standing strong (defense).

To ensure maximum offense, a single line seldom pressed forward by itself. Behind it were parallel lines, usually comprising thousands of soldiers, choreographed like ocean waves about to break on the beach. Likewise, on the defensive side, parallel lines of supporting troops intended to stop the breakers. If the front line cracked, a second, and a third, often came forward to seal the breach.

In theory, the strongest point of a defensive line is its center. That's where it's most dense, most compact, most difficult to break. For example, a football running play "up the gut" seldom succeeds other than to produce three-thousand-pound piles of prostrate players. The result of center strike in a Civil War battle was thousands of dead and wounded.

The weakest point of a defensive line is at its two ends—the right and left. The idea here (for the offense) is to go around a corner (hence the name "cornerback" in football) of the defensive line. The job of the cornerback is to hold the outside edge to ensure nothing can pass beyond the defensive line. If the defense fails, the offensive is said to have "flanked" the defense. A flanked defense may result in a big play, perhaps even a touchdown. On a Civil War battlefield, a flanked defensive line usually meant disaster—requiring the retreat of an entire army—and on the scoreboard, a guaranteed loss. The stakes, of course, could determine the destiny of a nation.

Now let's apply the principle of the line to Antietam.

The stadium is the Antietam Valley. The field is the rolling hills overlooking the Antietam Creek. The creek itself is the fifty yard line. But unlike on a flat football field—let's make it interesting—the creek has carved a canyon through the middle of the playing field. The creek forms a moat between the players, in this case, the U.S. Army and the Confederate Army. The opposing coaches are Robert E. Lee, representing the Stars and Bars, and George B. McClellan, singing The Star Spangled Banner.

As the teams (armies) arrive, something stands out that's quite noticeable. McClellan's team has his eleven players ready to go (a full complement on a football field). He also has a full bench, with even more reserves en route. Much of Lee's team is missing—only three players are visible. The rest haven't arrived at the stadium.

And when (or if) they do, Lee will be outnumbered, and his bench will be empty.

Remember the secret—the line. But your assumption was that the opposing lines of offense and defense were equal—the same in size and the same in length, with full parity. This is where the reality of war divorces itself from the paltriness of a game.

The lines weren't equal. McClellan had more men for his front line, more soldiers for his support lines and longer lines to extend his edges (flanks). Lee had fewer men, fewer lines and shorter lines. Odds were against him.

Still want to play, General Lee?

CHAPTER 26
Did McClellan Outthink Lee? Part II

Oh no, honey. I can't read little things like letters.
I read big things like men.
—Sojourner Truth[152]

GENERAL LEE DEVISED HIS GAME PLAN upon a fundamental tenet—cooperation of the enemy.

Evidence suggested this cooperation would not be forthcoming. Much to Lee's chagrin, the enemy refrained from lending support.

Lee's first miscalculation was that he anticipated "the grand armies of the United States" as "much weakened and demoralized" and "not yet organized," requiring "some time to prepare for the field."[153] Wrong on all counts.

Marse Robert's second bad assessment occurred when he entered Maryland with an expectation that her citizens would join him in "throwing off the oppression" of U.S. occupation. Didn't happen. "I do not anticipate any general rising of the people in our behalf," Lee was finally forced to conclude.[154]

Lee then erred in expecting the Federals to abandon the Shenandoah Valley and Harpers Ferry. They did not. "In this I was disappointed," he said.[155]

This setback required the issuance of Special Orders 191 to eradicate the Harpers Ferry menace. More misjudgment. Lee underestimated the time required for the complex maneuver, and he failed to acknowledge probable Union resistance. The resulting delays compelled Lee to direct, "It is necessary for you to abandon your position."[156]

The sudden appearance of an energized and reinvigorated U.S. army baffled Lee, forcing him to draw away from his main target—Pennsylvania—and retrograde to fight an unexpected defensive battle at South Mountain because "[T]he enemy was advancing more rapidly than was convenient."[157]

At South Mountain, Lee discovered himself outnumbered and outflanked. "I determined to withdraw," he noted.[158] The result: the first defeat of himself and his vaunted Army of Northern Virginia.

With his army in retreat, his forces divided and the enemy unexpectedly aggressive, Lee threw in the towel.

Antietam Creek, as viewed from the Union center. The Middle Bridge carried the Sharpsburg-Boonsboro Turnpike, and was one of three stone-arch bridges within close proximity of Sharpsburg. McClellan's flanking maneuver on September 16 crossed the Upper Bridge, about two miles upstream from this location.
Courtesy of the Library of Congress.

"The day has gone against us. This army will go by Sharpsburg and cross the river."[159] Invasion over.

Not a good record for General Lee. In the ten days since he invaded the United States, no wins—nothing but losses.

But even with his losing streak, Lee determined to make one more bet—George McClellan would not cross the Antietam Creek.

Lee's new plan depended—absolutely—on the Union army freezing as an ice sculpture on the opposite bank of the Antietam. A narrow moat with steep banks and sloping approaches, the Antietam, Lee believed, afforded just enough of a natural barricade to keep the Yankees away. This would provide Lee time—time to collect two-thirds of his Confederates from Harpers Ferry; time to reunite his army; time to reignite the invasion with a move northward from Sharpsburg. Lee deemed this doable.

Success, however, depended upon the absence of movements—the intractable inaction—of the enemy.

Lee's assumption was reasonable. General McClellan had a reputation for slowness, deliberateness and methodical plodding. Always believing himself outnumbered, he consistently hesitated, hoping for reinforcements, and awaiting perfect conditions before striking.

But Lee no longer was facing the McClellan who convulsed before Richmond. The George McClellan of mid-September had "all the plans of the [R]ebels" in his hands, believed he had "shockingly whipped" Lee at South Mountain, and determined he was pursuing toward the Potomac a wounded and fleeing foe in "rout and demoralization."[160]

Further emboldening McClellan—enemy numbers.

How's that? Hold on for a moment. Let's ruminate together. Isn't that a direct contradiction to everything we've learned about the disease "McClellanitis"?

Yes. But in this case, the disease works in McClellan's favor.

Explanation, please.

Let's return briefly to the Lost Order. The dispatch did not provide McClellan with numbers, but it did specify that two-thirds of the Confederate army was departing from Lee to strike at Harpers Ferry. By McClellan's math (and mine too), only one-third of the army remained with Lee.

So let's do a calculation, based upon McClellan's own estimates of Lee's strength:

120,000   (number of Rebels with the invasion force)
-80,000   (2/3 of the enemy army at Harpers Ferry)
 40,000   (with Lee at Sharpsburg)

Now let's recheck those numbers. Remember, McClellan is an engineer, who finished second in his West Point class. We must be certain of precision.

Incredible! Do you know what this means? McClellan outnumbers Lee!

For the moment.

McClellan knew he didn't have much time. Little Mac was aware Harpers Ferry had surrendered. He surmised (correctly) that Lee had called the Harpers Ferry victors to rejoin him. Union spies could see, from a signal post atop Red Hill, long lines of dust (thousands of marching men) moving from the Ferry in the direction of Sharpsburg. And McClellan deduced (correctly) that Lee was stalling—making a grand scene on the opposite bank of the Antietam, marching his inferior force back and forth, artillery bellowing, trying to dupe McClellan into a bad case of McClellanitis.

But McClellan wasn't buying. He knew—if he moved now—before Lee could unite and regain full strength—that he had the advantage. McClellan made his decision—we will cross the Antietam.

Now, where's the best passage?

Remember the "secret of the line"? (See previous chapter.) With his decision to advance, McClellan chose offense. Now as quarterback, he must decide where best to punch through the defensive line of Lee. Where was the weakness?

McClellan depended upon his scouts, topographic engineers, to provide him the answer. Keep in mind that McClellan had never viewed this ground. This was unknown territory. Neither he nor his generals had seen the Antietam Creek or visited nearby Sharpsburg. No USGS topo maps existed, and certainly he lacked the modern technology of today (GPS satellites, Lidar imagery, and Google Maps). So the topographic engineers spent Septem-

ber 15-16 exploring the landscape and probing the Confederate line of defense.

They discovered vulnerability.

Lee's left flank (the left edge of his line, or the point one mile north of Sharpsburg) was "in the air"; i.e., not anchored against a mountain, not protected by a river, not defended by a force. Lee had run out of men. He didn't have enough soldiers to extend his left far enough to prevent McClellan from crossing the Antietam—unopposed.

This presented an opportunity even better than South Mountain. There, too, McClellan had faced Lee's diminished strength; but he encountered stiff opposition as the Confederates fought for a day to defend the mountain passes. But here, along the Antietam, he had discovered a passage across the creek without enemy resistance. Incredible—and ideal.

McClellan subsequently commenced marching. He ordered nearly 20,000 soldiers—about one-third of his force—around the Confederate left on the afternoon and evening of September 16.

Lee learned of the maneuver through his vigilant cavalry; but he could do nothing, not anything, to stop it.

Lee's worst nightmare—McClellan was moving again, this time to Lee's side of the Antietam.

Another wrong bet.

CHAPTER 27

Redeemer's Road

Truth never yet fell dead in the streets;
it has such affinity with the soul of man,
the seed however broadcast will catch somewhere
and produce its hundredfold.
—Theodore Parker[161]

THE ROAD TO PENNSYLVANIA started at Sharpsburg.

This had not been General Lee's original intent. He had expected to utilize Hagerstown as his launch pad for his thrust into Pennsylvania. But the enemy had foiled that scheme, delaying the Confederates at Harpers Ferry and advancing aggressively at South Mountain.

Sharpsburg now became the focus of Lee's altered plans. But not for battle—concentration, instead. Once the Gray Fox reunited his army at Sharpsburg, he intended to drive north, with the Commonwealth of Pennsylvania in sight.

From Sharpsburg's rolling hills, one literally can see the Keystone State. As South Mountain stretches into the horizon, the ridge spans across the Mason Dixon Line. The geography map showed Lee located in the narrowest part of Maryland, where it funnels into an east-west hourglass. Lee knew the distance from Sharpsburg to the Pennsylvania border was only 15 miles—a one-day march for his bedraggled Confederate army.

The key to continuance of the invasion thus became the Sharpsburg-Hagerstown Turnpike. The red-clay road shot like an arrow due north for ten miles, terminating in the 18th century German settlement of Hagerstown. If Lee could move the army to Hagerstown, not only would Pennsylvania be in reach, he finally would establish linkage with the Confederate line of supply back to his home base of Winchester, Virginia.

Lee owned possession of the turnpike. He made certain of it, positioning a portion of his Sharpsburg defense along the road north of town. Lee comprehended the employment of that road as critical if his invasion were to continue. The general had experienced a week of setbacks, but momentum could be reclaimed and the Rebel dream of independence redeemed with a fresh surge north—upon that road.

Meanwhile, one mile distant, on the east side of the Antietam, paced General McClellan. No doubt the Union commander, too, knew about the Sharpsburg-Hagerstown Turnpike. Though a stranger to the area, he undoubtedly had access to the local Washington County map, freshly drawn in 1859, that clearly showed the road leading north.

The opportunity seemed obvious. What if McClellan could seize the road?

Little Mac didn't know Lee's thinking, but as a strategist, he certainly could surmise Lee's thoughts. McClellan had believed Pennsylvania a potential target from the outset of the invasion. McClellan knew Lee was concentrating at Sharpsburg, and he could interpret this two ways: Either Lee expected to fight there, or he intended to move from there. If McClellan could capture the road—and block Lee's avenue northward—he could eliminate the "move" option, with an outcome of forestalling invasion.

McClellan rose to the occasion. His flanking force seized the road! One of the most crucial junctures of the war (and I'm not hyperbolizing) occurred about two miles north of Sharpsburg on that late afternoon of September 16.

The U.S. commander cut off the enemy's line of advance into Pennsylvania. It represented the demise of Lee's invasion strategy. Remarkable. More amazing, McClellan accomplished this without battle, without skirmish, and barely firing a shot.

Sharpsburg's Main Street, looking west toward Shepherdstown. Situated between two ridges, the geographic "bottom of the bowl" that most of the town sits within helped protect it from the effects of the battle.
Courtesy of the Library of Congress.

(Note for Antietam students: The evening East Woods action is separate.)

Pause for a moment. Take a breather. Consider what just happened.

The most famous Confederate general of the Civil War has just been outsmarted, outflanked and outmaneuvered by the most debased Union general of the war. How can this be? Shouldn't I know this? Why is this unfamiliar?

Historians again.

Most Civil War historians grant McClellan zero credit for this extraordinary strategic success (I was in those ranks). Instead they focus on delay—they are determined to convince you of their dogma of delay—castigating McClellan for failing to pursue Lee aggressively after South Mountain; for failing to strike Lee immediately upon reaching the Antietam (September 15); and for not attacking with his full army on September 16. All of these delays enabled Lee to concentrate his strength, meaning McClellan missed exploiting him at the moment he was weakest.

In addition, these historians attempt to persuade you with their only acceptable outcome—the destruction of the Rebel army. September 16, in particular, was McClellan's big chance to effect the demolition of Lee and the end of the war.

Imbibe in the disparaging thinking of this trio of Antietam historians—Palfrey, Murfin & Sears—the most famous, most read and most popular writers on the topic.

"There is no censure too strong for his delay," Palfrey exclaimed. The Massachusetts lieutenant colonel, a veteran who fought and was wounded at Antietam, could not resist piling on: "It is an ungrateful task to be always finding fault, but . . . the perniciousness of the mistake which McClellan made in delaying his attack cannot be too strongly insisted upon."[162]

In support of the destruction theme, Palfrey observed: "[Lee] was in a position from which he could not hope to escape without serious fighting and serious loss, but he had not to fear destruction unless his opponent struck at once and struck hard." Palfrey flourished his critique with this uppercut knockout: "If [McClellan] had used the priceless hours . . . as he might have, his name would have stood high in the roll of commanders."[163]

Civil War centennial historian Murfin was not as effusive, but equally blunt: "Once again McClellan was obliging [Lee]," critiqued Murfin. "He was giving [away] time . . . McClellan, and he alone, was bringing the odds down, and down, and down." Murfin concluded: "Lee made the best of every advantage offered him; McClellan tossed away every one Lee gave him."[164]

Two decades following Murfin, Stephen Sears offered his own assessments. McClellan "plodded through the day," perhaps missing "the best chance of all." Sears scolded McClellan for his cautiousness, resulting in ineptitude: "Rather than act he would only react, and in this peculiar attitude of command [across from Lee along the Antietam], he surrendered much of the initiative to his opponent."[165]

When Robert E. Lee lost the Sharpsburg-Hagerstown Turnpike—his road into Pennsylvania—his arrow of invasion—as a result of a deliberate and calculated maneuver by his enemy—do you think General Lee believed McClellan had surrendered much of the initiative to his opponent?

McClellan's capture of that road on September 16 forced Lee into a sorry predicament. Now blocked and unable to move northward, the Confederate commander succumbed to two choices, neither of them good: One, fight another unwelcome battle, at an unwanted time, at an undesired location; or two, retreat into Virginia, return home, yet again canceling the invasion.

George McClellan expected Lee to be reasonable. The Rebels would retire. Victory was his. Joyous with his achievement, McClellan telegraphed his wife Mary Ellen on the 16th: "[H]ave no doubt delivered Penn[sylvania] and Maryland. All well and in excellent spirits."[166]

McClellan had discovered his road to redemption.

But history never noticed.

CHAPTER 28
Blinders

How much intellect has been employed
mousing after texts, to sustain preconceived doctrine.
—Lydia M. Child[167]

ONE OF MY FAVORITE MEMORIES is riding my grandfather's draft horse, Old Fleet.

Old Fleet was a powerful animal, meant for plowing fields, and not for horseback riding. But my grandfather Poffenberger, who owned a farm on South Mountain, used to pick me up and plant me on the midsection of Old Fleet's spine, where I rode like a medieval knight, swatting away prehistoric and gigantic horse flies.

For hours we would plow up and down, back and forth, through hundreds of rows of black raspberries—a devious but delectable fruit native to the slopes of South Mountain. We would stop only to permit Old Fleet to deposit a few "warm biscuits," but otherwise, the horse plodded along, seeing nothing beyond her blinders.

While enjoying my reminiscence of a half-century ago, I began pondering the origin of "blinders." A quick visit to the Merriam-Webster dictionary informed me that the word originated about 1807. Mr. Noah Webster—known for Americanizing (simplifying) the King's English by changing "centre" to "center" and "colour" to "color"—gave us two definitions for blinders. First, the horse's; i.e., why are these leather things attached to my bridle preventing me from viewing my normal field of vision; and second, the human's—a limitation or obstruction to sight or discernment.

Blinders affect us all, often taking the form of bull-headedness. You know what I mean—the attitude of, "I know I'm right; don't challenge me on this; end of discussion." Every couple on the planet has encountered this example of blinders. Blinders are conditioned by point of view and stance—or stated more simply, this is the way it was; this is the way it is; and this is the way it will be.

Historians, who occasionally admit they do sometimes devolve into their human psyche, must beware of blinders. They must possess open minds and wide-open eyes as they scan sources, always on alert for injections of opinion—and most dangerous, "truisms" presented as points of view. A cardinal error of the historian is acceptance, rather than challenge.

A classic case of historian blinders occurs at the commencement of the Battle of Antietam. The blinders are this—historians have assumed both Lee and McClellan wanted their fight at Antietam.

Not so.

Actions, indeed, forced the two generals into combat, but both hoped to avoid conflict along the Antietam. A battle, at that place and at that time, didn't further their aims.

Lee's aim, of course, was the invasion of Pennsylvania. McClellan had made that impossible, at least via a road from Sharpsburg. Lee determined to make a stand at Sharpsburg only after McClellan removed his invasion option. And here's where historians are shackled by blinders.

Most Civil War historians accept the "We will make our stand on these hills" principle as fact. We've debunked that pedigree (see Chapter 5). Nowhere, in any of Lee's contemporary messages to President Davis or his subordinate generals prior to September 17, does he indicate a determination to stand and fight at Antietam. We've established why Lee remained at Sharpsburg (recall the four-letter words in Chapter 23); and how McClellan disrupted this program with his unexpected and undesired crossing of the Antietam (last chapter).

An assertion by Stephen Sears that Lee "was not being forced into battle against his will" (opinion); and that "he chose

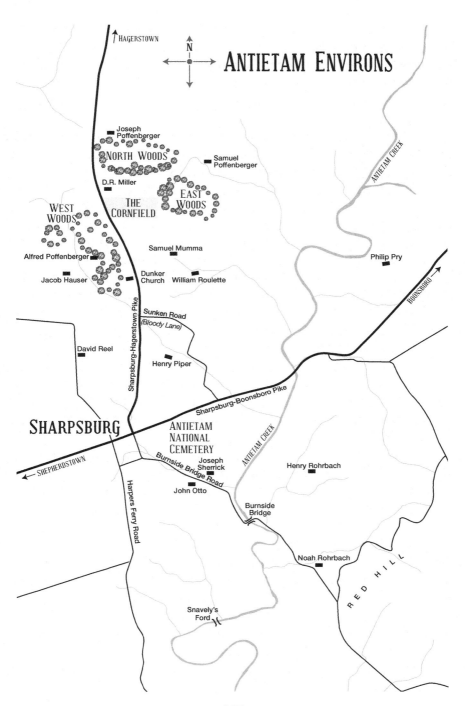

ANTIETAM ENVIRONS

his ground deliberately" (opinion); is unsupported by anything that Lee wrote.[168] For decades, I concurred with Sears. But I've discerned my error. Other historians have repeated the same misinterpretation—somehow Lee was in control of his destiny. "It was almost as if Lee was pulling the strings of a Federal puppet" (opinion courtesy of James Murfin).[169]

Blinders. Blinders. Circumstances had forced Lee into a box. Lee was not baiting McClellan. McClellan had trapped Lee. Why has that been so hard for historians (including me) to see?

The Confederate commander did have one escape route—retreat back into Virginia—but that seemed unpalatable. Virginia was opposite the direction of Pennsylvania; the wrong way for continuance of the invasion. If Lee departed without a fight, he lost all momentum at best; and at worst, he handed the U.S. a psychological victory. Lee, the consummate boxer who stampeded the ring rather than dancing on the ropes, determined his course— battle his way out. But that was not a predetermined decision, as characterized otherwise by historians, who have been victimized over and again by their suspect sources.

McClellan, for his part, expected Lee to go home. He wanted Lee to leave. If Lee returned to Virginia, McClellan was the winner. Lee's very departure from Sharpsburg—and the Confederate withdrawal from Northern territory—meant victory for the Union commander.

To help ensure this happy outcome, McClellan purposely—intentionally—showed his hand to his enemy on the afternoon and evening of September 16. First, by seizing the Sharpsburg-Hagerstown Turnpike (Lee's avenue north); and second, by attacking Lee.

Actually, it was more like a whack than an attack. The first Federal forces across the Antietam tested Lee's left flank as dusk neared, scouting its location and strength. This brief encounter no doubt pleased Little Mac, for it made Lee fully aware that the Yankees, in strength, were now on the Confederate side of the Antietam. To further this point, the Federals displayed a full corps of Bluecoats within a half-mile of the Rebels. McClellan was delivering a message to Lee: I'm coming after you. Leave now, while you can.

It was not a bluff. McClellan was preparing for battle. In fact, he sent a second army corps across the Antietam later that evening to bolster the strength of his own position (now nearly 20,000 men). But if the bullying by itself could work—convincing Lee that he meant business, resulting in a Rebel retreat—perhaps he could avoid battle. Every army commander dreams about defeating the enemy through maneuver in lieu of battle. That's the zenith of military brilliance.

Not according to Antietam historians. McClellan blundered. He announced himself. He exposed himself to the enemy. He lost all advantage of surprise. According to Sears: "General McClellan was telegraphing his punch."[170]

Blinders! In fairness to Sears, he did not invent this charge. The champion of this canard was Francis Palfrey.

Writing twenty years after the battle, and with ample time for reflection, Palfrey accused McClellan of malpractice. "[H]e should not tell his opponent what he was going to do," argued Palfrey. "Able commanders seek to delude their opponents." He continued, "They use all the craft which they possess to induce the enemy to believe that the blow is to fall at some place other than the place which they have chosen."[171]

Palfrey is correct. These are fundamental tenets of war. But Palfrey is not considering Machiavellian tactics, which in this case meant employing obvious definition, rather than deception, as the method of outsmarting your enemy.

Failing to grasp this prospect (blinders!), and exasperated with his former commander, Palfrey concluded: "But McClellan resorted to no such artifices; on the contrary, he informed Lee."[172]

Precisely my point—he informed Lee intentionally—bullying him to leave; shoving him to go home.

Unfortunately for George McClellan, General Lee did not take kindly to bullying.

CHAPTER 29
Shakespearean Stage

*Exaggerated history is poetry and truth
referred to a new standard.*
—Henry David Thoreau[173]

WHAT'S YOUR BEST INSURANCE against refutation of a criticism?

Ensure the target of the criticism is dead.

I'm not suggesting murder. Natural causes will suffice. A guaranteed way to cement your impressions upon history is to outlive your rivals. With the criticized individual in the grave, the last word belongs to the critic.

This rule is an absolute. What should not be absolute, however, is the legitimacy and truth assigned to these last words by non-discerning historians.

Civil War histories are replete with these types of falsehoods, as old soldiers engage in revisionist histories, cleverly told, to make themselves look better. I'm guilty of buying their tales myself. The story is just too juicy; the critique right on point; the drama perfectly intense; the quotation exactly right. Each of these is a hidden trap, not easily avoided, because they appeal to our emotions. We thrive on conflict, real or not. We demand protagonists and antagonists. Otherwise, we have no story.

The historian's task, however, is not simply to tell the story. We must be vigilant of the storytellers.

Antietam's Bloody Lane illustrated this case. The battle had been raging for almost four hours before action commenced at the Sunken Road. Thus far it had been an excellent morning for General McClellan, and near disaster for Robert E. Lee. U.S. forces had collapsed Lee's left around The Cornfield; captured his left center at the Dunker Church; and driven the Rebels into the West Woods. Lee was nearing a breaking point, exacerbated by the continued absence of much of his Army, not yet arrived from Harpers Ferry. A dramatic moment occurred when Rebel reinforcements arrived just in time to salvage the West Woods line (Lee's readjusted left).[174]

Then attention shifted to Lee's right center—a sunken dirt farm road enclosed with zigzag split-rail fencing—forever re-titled Bloody Lane.

For nearly four hours, the Confederates fended off intermittent assaults against this natural fortification. The slaughter on either side unimaginable—nearly 6,000 Americans dead or wounded and bleeding (equal to our casualties on D-Day). The Federal waves finally became too much, and by early afternoon, the Rebel defense collapsed. The climax—the Confederate center was breached. Oh no!

Let the grandstanding begin.

The first to exaggerate the outcome of this affair were two Southern generals. Daniel Harvey (D.H.) Hill (the same culprit whose headquarters lost Lee's orders one week earlier), held, then lost, the Bloody Lane position. "Affairs looked critical," the general claimed in his after-action report. Following two failed attempts to secure the break with several hundred rallied refugees, Hill nevertheless surmised this had "a most happy effect" because "The Yankees were completely deceived by their boldness, and induced to believe there was a large force in our center. They made no further attempt to pierce our center."[175]

This one could qualify for Aesop's Fables. I don't doubt Hill's miniature counter-offenses, but to accept his notion that these fanciful displays scared and deluded the U.S. army? Wouldn't you know. Antietam historians have eagerly embraced this tale—and repeated it over and again. Why?

Confederate dead in the Bloody Lane.
Courtesy of the Library of Congress.

Even Hill's boss, General James Longstreet, found Hill's story too exaggerated to repeat. But he reinforced the mantra—"From this moment our center was extremely weak." He then related how one small regiment from North Carolina (the 27th) stood before the enemy's masses about one-quarter mile from the Bloody Lane, "being without a cartridge. . . . [The colonel] stood with his empty guns, and waved his colors to show that his troops were in position."

151

After 90 minutes or so, with the aid of close-range Rebel artillery, the Federal lines "began to hesitate, soon halted, and . . . retired."[176]

I do not doubt this story. Nor do I discount the bravery of these Tarheels. I do not have the courage they displayed. What requires censure, though, is Longstreet's implication that this stand stopped the momentum of Union assaults. A ridiculous notion. But once again, a yarn too good for the historian's critique. The result is its repetition, ad nauseam.

And here's my very favorite. "Lee's army was ruined and the end of the Confederacy in sight."[177]

These are the eternal words of Lee's ordnance officer, Edward Porter Alexander. These words are so powerful, so visual, so shocking, that the National Park Service featured them as the bold introductory title on the exhibit that explained the action at Bloody Lane. No doubt millions of battlefield visitors have contemplated those words while standing in awe at that sacred site. The script is complete; the connotation obvious—why doesn't McClellan exploit this breach? It's his opportunity to end the war.

I, myself, embraced Alexander's words. I so enjoyed guiding my tour groups to that exhibit, where I asked them, in unison, to repeat those fateful words with me. The moment was high drama. It deserved a Shakespearean second.

I then condemned McClellan as a moral coward. I chastised him for refusing to rush the gap with fresh reserves. I emphasized my point, describing a parallel scene occurring one mile distant, on the opposite side of the Antietam. McClellan was contemplating commitment of his reserves, when his favorite subordinate confronted him with this warning: "Remember, General! I command the last reserve of the last Army of the Republic."[178] McClellan melted.

Two remarkable stories, huh? Both of them untrue.

Some years ago when conducting research on Harpers Ferry, I inadvertently discovered E. P. Alexander was not at Antietam. He was miles away at the Ferry gathering captured ammunition and ordnance. He wasn't present on the field to witness one shot of the battle. How could he know "the end of the Confederacy was in sight"?

Turns out Alexander penned those fateful words long after the war, in his military memoirs in 1907—nearly a half-century after the battle.[179] After berating myself for my own stupid error, I brought this to the attention of my National Park Service peers, and to their credit, the misleading exhibit was removed. Unfortunately, that does not erase the indelible impression imprinted upon the minds of millions of visitors.

Even the warning to McClellan—the one about "last reserve of the last Army" is suspect. Its source is a Union officer, writing to *The Century Magazine* in 1886, almost a quarter-century after the battle. His letter appears as a footnote in an article about Antietam. Though present on battle day (by his telling, within 150 yards of McClellan), he, himself, did not hear this conversation. In fact, he heard it second hand, at some unknown date after the war, from another officer.[180] Can you believe I once believed this as gospel?

McClellan, incidentally, had died the year before the writing of this letter.

And that brings me to my final example. Even a best friend of McClellan's—concerning this topic of advancing the reserves— could not resist his self-discovery of long-missing courage following McClellan's death.

General William B. Franklin, a stalwart defender of Little Mac during the war, wrote in an 1887 article in *The Century Magazine* about his arrival at Antietam. He recalled deploying opposite the Dunker Church nearly six hours after the battle had opened, watching intently as the West Woods in front of him filled with Rebel infantry and supporting artillery. When McClellan arrived to assess the situation, according to the article, Franklin informed him: "I thought the attack ought to be made."[181] McClellan refused.

Oh come on, General Franklin. You're the one who claimed, only three days before, while on your cautious approach to Harpers Ferry: "They outnumber me two to one. I shall wait here until I learn the prospect for re-enforcement."[182] And in that case, the Confederates were in full view. At Antietam, the woods disguised your vision, making you, no doubt, even more uncomfortable. Yet you were insisting upon attack? Amazing how Franklin's timidity turned into fortitude over the course of 25 years.

Sorry to say, this Franklin saga also has been repeated time and again. We historians just can't seem to figure it out.

But none of these infractions of history are the biggest scandals of Antietam.

The largest lie of all was elsewhere.

CHAPTER 30

Framed

People do not seem to realize that their opinion of the world
is also a confession of character.
—Ralph Waldo Emerson[183]

IT'S ONE OF THE MOST AWFUL experiences in our lives.

Your best friend turns against you.

The person you've trusted and most admired, someone you truly respected. The companion you've spent the most time with and shared your innermost feelings. Your friend, you thought, for a lifetime—the one and only "BBF."

Then, suddenly, for whatever reason, the mutual admiration explodes. Your best regresses into your worst. Your world has been rocked.

Two of Antietam's most famous generals—George McClellan and Ambrose Burnside—were best buds. "Mac" and "Burn," as they affectionately dubbed each other, had attended West Point together. Burnside showed promise as an inventor, developing the first U.S. military weapon to utilize a metallic cartridge; but his initial venture failed, forcing him into bankruptcy. McClellan rescued his friend in the decade before the Civil War, offering him a good position with McClellan's Illinois Central Railroad.

When the Civil War erupted, and President Lincoln appointed McClellan to command his armies, McClellan entrusted Burnside

General Ambrose E. Burnside.
Courtesy of the Library of Congress.

with one of his most important assignments—organizing and training the raw recruits. Burnside soon tired, however, of being a "glorified drillmaster." He wanted action. In early 1862, he gained distinction as commander of the Coast Division, leading an invasion that brought him headlines for blocking a majority of the

North Carolina coast from Confederate shipping. McClellan was thrilled. "My friend Burnside has so far done splendidly," he informed his mother.[184]

After the war's first year, the only general with more successes than Burnside was U.S. Grant.

Lincoln noticed. So impressed was the president with Burnside's accomplishments, when he fired McClellan after his failure to seize Richmond, Lincoln offered Burnside command of McClellan's former army. Burnside refused. Lincoln offered again when Lee's invasion commenced. Burnside again demurred, suggesting his friend McClellan was more able, more competent and more confident. "I know Burnside to be true to me," McClellan once confided to his wife Mary Ellen. "[T]here can be no doubt about that."[185]

McClellan so trusted Burnside, that when the emergency of Lee's invasion struck, he entrusted Burnside with the maneuver to protect Baltimore; to lead pursuit of the enemy toward Frederick; and to command the force attempting the breakthrough at South Mountain. McClellan believed in Burnside.

Until . . .

"I ought to rap Burnside very severely & probably will," he complained to his wife. "He is very slow & is not fit to command more than a regiment. If I rap him as he deserves he will be my mortal enemy hereafter."[186]

What happened?

Another friend arrived who broke up the dynamic duo. Ever had that happen to you?

The man was Fitz-John Porter. You know you're dealing with a character when the hyphen is for his first name, and not his last. Porter adored McClellan. He deemed himself Little Mac's greatest defender. Friend, confidant and most staunch loyalist, Porter reaped rewards, with McClellan elevating him to the status of being his favorite general. Porter "stuck through it all most nobly," McClellan shared with his wife when addressing Porter's commitment. "He is all that I thought him & more. Nothing has depressed him; he is always cheerful, active & ready, & is much more efficient than all put together."[187]

Who wouldn't want a best friend like that?

But Porter soon found trouble. Not long after McClellan's firing, Porter was charged with treason (loyalty to person above loyalty to country). He was accused of delay and delinquency for intentionally failing to render timely assistance to another U.S. army fighting near Washington (that army was defeated at Second Manassas). He was arrested and was awaiting trial in Washington when the Rebel invasion began.[188]

McClellan begged for his release. During the emergency, he contended, he needed Porter's experience as a general. McClellan persisted. Reluctantly, authorities relented (for the moment). Porter subsequently rushed to McClellan, rejoining his comrade as the Battle of South Mountain raged. In addition to bringing thousands of troops, Porter brought shocking news.

Burnside was the cause of his treason charges!

At that moment, General McClellan welded himself to Porter and divorced forever Ambrose Burnside.

Subsequent actions revealed the split-up. First, the victor of South Mountain (Burnside) received no credit for his victory when McClellan reported to Washington. Not one mention of "Burn." Then Burnside was charged with delay in pursuing the enemy from South Mountain, as McClellan ordered Porter to shove him aside and to take the lead. Then, once along the Antietam, Burnside was accused of delay in taking proper position.

Notice the pattern—delay, delay, delay. Were McClellan and Porter projecting their own faults upon Burnside?

"I am instructed to call upon you for explanations of these failures," an aide wrote on McClellan's behalf. "[I]n view of the important military operations at hand, the commanding general cannot lightly regard such marked departure from the tenor of his instructions."[189]

Ouch. Talk about a punch in the gut. And for exclamation, McClellan relieved Burnside as his only wing commander while en route from South Mountain to Sharpsburg—a designation he had held since the army departed Washington.[190]

Bruised, battered and bewildered—the fall from friend to foe had occurred at a dizzying pace—Burnside sent a let's-make-up note, written in a formal third-person, general-to-general format, to McClellan's Antietam headquarters.

"General Burnside . . . is sorry to have received so severe a rebuke from the general commanding" (translation—what did I do to upset you?). "[H]e is particularly sorry that the general commanding feels that his instructions have not been obeyed" (translation—I beg you for forgiveness). ["N]othing can occur to prevent the general from continuing his hearty cooperation to the best of his ability" (translation—we can work this out, Mac).[191]

Too late. McClellan tossed Burnside into the rubbish pile, condemning him for the troubles of his best friend Fitz-John Porter. Guilty, incidentally, was the verdict against Porter later on. But not because Burnside had conspired against him. "Burn" simply had been an innocent intermediary, passing Porter's own poisonous and incendiary words on to Washington, without censure.

Fitz-John Porter.
Courtesy of the Library of Congress.

Historians have viewed this spat with interest. Of course we have. More drama—nothing better than a fight between best friends on the eve of the battle that may determine the nation's destiny.

The conventional narrative adopted by most Antietam historians is that Burnside began pouting and plotting vengeance against his former pal. Historian James Murfin noted Burnside's "disgruntled attitude," and "spite," positing that Burnside failed to reconnoiter his position intentionally, doing "only as he was told and no more." Stephen Sears explained Burnside's "demotion" as wing commander, hinting of incompetence. He then described Burnside as "rankled" and with "ruffled feathers," adopting an unusual demeanor for the "normally genial and uncomplaining officer."[192]

Burnside certainly was confused and confounded by this unexpected and unexplained treatment on the part of his friend. But Burnside was not boorish, nor irksome, nor childish. Those were McClellan characteristics.

Meanwhile, at Antietam, McClellan hitched Porter to his headquarters, comforted by his loyalty and dependent upon his advice. As Little Mac executed his grand flanking maneuver around Lee's left on September 16—the move he hoped would grant him his grand victory—he kept Burnside idle, three miles south, where he could have nothing to do with Little Mac's glorious moment.

But the moment spurred McClellan—and then seized Burnside.

CHAPTER 31
Deceived

For the Lie, as a Virtue, a Principle,
is eternal; the Lie . . . man's best and surest friend,
is immortal, and cannot perish from the earth.
—Mark Twain[193]

LYING IS THE ORIGINAL human sport.

Lying is second, only behind the temptation to disobedience, as the original sin. God did not create us as liars; He did not implant us with a liar's gene. We invented the concept ourselves. "Lying is universal—we all do it," mused Mark Twain. "Therefore, the wise thing is for us diligently to train ourselves to lie thoughtfully, judiciously; to lie with a good object, and not an evil one."[194]

The purpose of the lie is to dupe a person, making one (or the many, if the liar happens to be a politician) believe the untrue is true. Those who fall for the lie we define as fools. No one has escaped the honorary title of fool.

There are three types of liars. The apprentice liar is unpolished, unpracticed and unconvincing. The apprentice infrequently utilizes the lie, and usually with poor results. The journeyman liar is more practiced, employing the trade more often, and with much better success. Then we have the master liar—one who can conquer us completely in a sentence, a paragraph or a tweet.

The success of a lie is determined in two ways: One, in its believability, and two, the liar's escape from culpability. Here is where almost everyone fails. It's easy to create a lie; it's hard to maintain it without losing your cover. Lies are like stacking dominoes, with each succeeding lie dependent upon a shakier and more baseless foundation. Few possess the patience, perseverance and petulance necessary to prevent the prostration of the lie.

Every great leader in American history has been a liar, some more so than others. The Civil War, too, has an abundance of liars. My favorites are generals and colonels who wrote reports, using euphemisms (lies) to explain their rapid departure (retreat) from the field: "Our ammunition expended;" the men "fatigued from the fight;" "our weapons old and becoming jammed." These are colorful explanations for withdrawal, each attempting to avoid the truth.

Antietam's greatest liar is George Brinton McClellan. I do not say this to criticize McClellan, but to compliment him. McClellan expended considerable thought in the construction of believable lies. We should reward the general for his creative genius rather than scold him for childish and churlish behavior.

My complaint is not with McClellan as a liar, but with historians who have not detected his lies. Every quality historian is a Sherlock Holmes. Our job is detection of untruths in our ad infinitum pursuit of truth. At Antietam, McClellan has duped historians. He has convinced us of his own confusion, when we, in fact, are confused.

As example, we accept McClellan's plan for battle as truth. It is a fabrication—brilliantly contrived by the general after the battle. In other words, the fight occurred first; then McClellan conceived his plan, ensuring his design matched the circumstances of the fight. This approach guaranteed McClellan command control. He made it appear that he had devised his plan from the outset, and that any deviation was not his fault. Machiavellian perfection!

The truth is otherwise. McClellan did have one plan—scaring Lee away without a fight. McClellan intended his forceful move against Lee's left flank on the evening of September 16 to be so convincing, so compelling, that Lee would retreat back into Virginia. Lee's withdrawal from the North, in itself, constituted victory for McClellan.

View of Burnside Bridge from the high ground
held by the Confederates.
Courtesy of the Library of Congress.

But Lee refused the offer. Instead of departure, he stood his ground. As the sun rose on Wednesday morning, September 17, and the U.S. army discovered Lee steadfastly holding his ground, McClellan had to revert to Plan B. But Plan B was not a plan, it was a reaction—continuous reaction. It was not preconceived, but a response— a day of response, determined by circumstances throughout the action.

McClellan, though, has successfully convinced us over the past 150-plus years that he carefully prepared this predetermined plan. Here it is:

"The design was to make the main attack upon the enemy's left—at least to create a diversion in favor of the main attack, with the hope of something more by assailing the enemy's right—and, as soon as one or both of the flank movements were fully successful, to attack their center with any reserve I might then have on hand."[195]

Huh?

Let me check. Is that written in English? Let's reread—slowly. It's still not making much sense. Pardon my confused neurons. What, exactly, is the plan?

Permit me to attempt an interpretation. McClellan's plan included three components: 1. Strike Lee's left. 2. Strike Lee's right, simultaneously in coordination with the strike on the left. 3. Follow up with an assault up the middle.

Let's visualize this in the boxing ring. McClellan intends to smash Lee's skull with simultaneous blows from his right and left fists, then knock him out with a jab into his gut.

Really? Is this practical?

Consider the difficulty of coordinating your fists so that they pound the sides of your opponent's face at precisely the same time. Then contemplate this: Your right hand and left hands are detached, separated by nearly three miles. They cannot see each other. Hills and valleys and the Antietam Creek separate your fists. You have no instantaneous communication, so it's impossible to coordinate the punches. Oh, incidentally, not only are your fists detached. Your entire body's been bisected and scattered—the right part is across the Antietam, while the left part still must cross the creek.

This picture (plan) is ludicrous. McClellan calmly and convincingly presents it, however, in his post-battle report, prepared four weeks after the battle. A masterful lie.

Historians have discovered no pre-battle orders written by McClellan that confirm this plan. Good generals usually wrote good orders to ensure clarity and precision in execution. Perhaps that's the best confirmation that McClellan had no battle plan.

Evidence does suggest, however, that McClellan had a firm plan for the protection of his own left flank.

Hold on a moment. I thought McClellan's attention was on the enemy's left flank.

Correct. McClellan did assail Lee's left, with the hope of encouraging him to flee from the field.

But McClellan had his own flank to worry about—his vulnerable left. Recall the "secret of the line" (Chapter 25). The greatest danger the Confederates posed to McClellan's own line was to his left. McClellan first arrived along the Antietam on September 15—the same day that the Confederates had captured Harpers Ferry. McClellan knew about the surrender. He also witnessed Lee stalling at Sharpsburg. McClellan likely used his West Point acumen to make this judgment—the Rebels intended to reunite at Sharpsburg.

This prospect presented a bad scenario. The most direct north-south route for the Confederates to approach Sharpsburg was via the Harpers Ferry-Sharpsburg Road. McClellan certainly knew of this road, as the U.S. cavalry utilized it as its avenue of escape from Harpers Ferry. This rural dirt byway, also used by John Brown three years before, created a hazardous situation—it ran directly into McClellan's underbelly (his left).

Worse still, the road was situated on the same side of the Antietam occupied by McClellan. In other words, the creek paralleled the road to its west. Upon the east bank stood McClellan. Thus McClellan could not depend upon the Antietam as a natural barrier between his position and any Confederates approaching from the south (Harpers Ferry).

McClellan surmised (correctly) that the Rebels were coming to Sharpsburg, but he didn't know their route. If they advanced via the quickest and shortest approach, Stonewall Jackson, along with two-thirds of the Confederate army, would be pouncing upon McClellan's left flank.

This dangerous situation required attention. To protect his endangered left, McClellan chose Burnside—the only man in his army who had exercised independent command of an army.

McClellan entrusted the defense of his most vulnerable position to the venerable Burnside. In essence, McClellan had Burnside construct a dam of Bluecoats on a ridge overlooking the Noah Rohrbach farm, about two miles south of Sharpsburg. This position was ideal for defense. It featured a steep vertical bluff, running perpendicular to the Antietam, connecting the creek bank with the base of Red Hill mountain. It presented a natural fortress that best protected McClellan's left flank.

Here Burnside stood, vigilant and strong, facing south toward Harpers Ferry, on September 16. McClellan was ready for any Rebels approaching Sharpsburg.

But not a single Confederate would come that way. Jackson selected a more secure and safer route through Virginia, virtually guaranteeing reunification with Lee without opposition.

Only after McClellan convinced himself that the Rebels weren't threatening his left did he design alternate plans for General Burnside to attack at the stone bridge. Only then did McClellan decide to assail Lee's right.

Any notion otherwise is a lie.

CHAPTER 32
Betrayed

Greatness lies, not in being strong,
But in the right using of strength;
and strength is not used rightly when it serves
only to carry a man above his fellows
for his own glory.
—Henry Ward Beecher[196]

GEORGE MCCLELLAN WON the Battle of Antietam.
But his critics claimed he lost.

The dawn-to-dusk slugfest on September 17 killed or maimed more than 23,000 Americans—equal to total American casualties in the Revolutionary War, the War of 1812 and Mexican War combined. The bruised Confederates eventually departed Sharpsburg, limping gingerly out of Maryland and returning home to Virginia and the Confederacy.

McClellan held the field. The enemy had retreated. This, by definition, was victory. "Those in whose judgment I rely tell me that I fought the battle splendidly," he gleefully wrote his wife Mary Ellen on the morning following the fight. " . . . that it was a masterpiece of art."[197]

Two days later he effused with success: "Thank Heaven for one thing—my military reputation is cleared." Little Mac then shared the sweetest words with his wife. "I have shown that I can fight battles & win them!" Husband George then delivered his denouement. "I think my enemies are pretty effectively killed by this time! May they remain so!!"[198]

These "enemies" were not Confederates. They were President Lincoln; the president's cabinet; the War Department; General-in-Chief Halleck; the Republican Congress; Republican generals; Republican officers; Republican editors; and the Republican press. In sum, everyone in the United States who dared to question General McClellan (most of them Republicans).

But still there were doubters. McClellan, indeed, had defeated Lee, but defeat was not the end game. Destruction of Lee's Army must be the outcome—annihilation of the Rebels the result.

General Joseph Hooker, who had led McClellan's swing against Lee's left during the battle, exemplified this negating attitude about McClellan—though the winner, actually a loser.

In a conversation with the secretary of treasury in Washington one week after the battle, Hooker was "very free in his expressions about McClellan." Wounded in the battle and now recovering in the capital, Hooker explained that he thought Little Mac "not fit to lead a great army; that he is timid and hesitating when decision is necessary; that the battle of Antietam was near being lost by his way of fighting." Hooker concluded the victory was incomplete. He told the secretary "the defeat of the enemy should have been final."[199]

This chorus of criticism continued to a crescendo. The reputation McClellan believed he had restored at Antietam, in its aftermath, degenerated once again into ill-repute.

This required a loud response.

Eleven months after the battle, in August 1863, McClellan issued his final report on the campaign. The document became his bearer of self-defense, arguing with passion and persuasion that he had saved Washington, preserved Pennsylvania, and ridded Maryland of an invading Rebel army. But in acknowledgment of the furor that the Confederate Army had escaped, McClellan devised his excuse.

Burnside.

General Burnside was an easy target. He, himself, had a ruined reputation by the time McClellan prepared his official report. Burnside bore blame for the debacle of a U.S. defeat at the Battle of Fredericksburg, three months following Antietam. Even better for McClellan, he could tarnish the general who had replaced him. (Lincoln had hoisted Burnside into the commander's chair, firing Little Mac seven weeks after Antietam.) No one now was defending Burnside; no one was touting him; there was agreement he had been a disaster as army commander. If McClellan could blame Burnside for his failure to destroy Lee at Antietam, Burnside appeared ripe for the picking.

To accomplish this, McClellan injected three intentional lies into his official report, all accusing Burnside of "delay." Specifically, he leveled three charges against Burnside: 1. Delay in execution of an attack order; 2. delay in seizing the target, and 3. delay in staging a grand assault.

McClellan contended that each one of these pauses proved fatal, collectively dooming his opportunity to destroy Lee. But each charge was a charade, contrived by a conniving conspirator who lacked consideration for a former friend and moral conscience for a fellow army commander.

Before examining these charges, however, we must first consider the context. When Lee refused to budge (as McClellan had hoped), Little Mac launched an attack, using his right wing as the boxer. The left, where Burnside stood, remained quiet, other than artillery exchange. This suited McClellan, as Burnside was serving as an anchor for the right wing as it was swinging against the Rebel left.

After about 3½ hours, the situation became so desperate for General Lee on his left that he required reinforcements. Subsequently, about 9 a.m., Lee pulled most of the Confederates opposite Burnside's position (where no action was underway).[200] This move of nearly 4,000 Rebels occurred right beneath the nose of U.S. signalmen atop Red Hill mountain. It was impossible to miss. Though we don't have the original message, we know McClellan was informed. Concerned that Lee was shifting resources, McClellan needed to apply pressure against the Rebel right. Thus, at 9:10 a.m. (ten minutes after the Confederates began hastening away from that sector), he wrote an order to Burnside instructing him to attack. Minutes ticked by as the order went through the arduous process of delivery. By 10 a.m., Burnside's troops were in motion.

Their target was a three-arch stone bridge spanning the Antietam Creek, foreverafter known as Burnside Bridge.

That's the actuality. But here's McClellan's version:

Charge No. 1: Burnside delayed the attack until three hours after he was ordered. Burnside resisted, despite three different entreaties from McClellan's personal emissaries, delivering orders "to assault the bridge at once, and carry it at all hazards." The false statement here was that Burnside delayed after receiving orders. Not true.

Charge No. 2: Burnside failed to promptly take the bridge. "After three [more] hours delay, the bridge was carried at 1 o'clock by a brilliant charge." It did take three hours, but Burnside was not idle. He conducted a flanking maneuver (over difficult terrain and fording the Antietam), that brought U.S. troops to the rear of the enemy defending the bridge. Once the maneuver was completed, the Rebels fled. The falsehood here was that Burnside wasted time seizing the bridge.

Myth Moment: It's a myth that Burnside hammered and hammered the bridge with frontal assaults. He forced the Confederate abandonment of the position primarily by going around it. Don't believe me? Check out the casualties. Burnside carried the bridge with the fewest U.S. casualties of anywhere else on the battlefield.

Charge No. 3: Burnside halted for two hours once he controlled the bridge. Yes, but for the purpose of moving three divisions (9,000 infantrymen) through a 12-foot wide funnel across a stone bridge. Twenty-two cannon pulled by 132 horses also crammed through the narrow passage. Once across the creek, Burnside required time to deploy his men in a one-mile-wide line—the largest coordinated attack of the day. McClellan's fabrication here: Burnside dawdled most of the afternoon away.

"Had this important movement been consummated two hours earlier," McClellan fibbed, "[o]ur victory might thus have been much more decisive."[201]

Slam dunk! It's all Burnside's fault. Those unnecessary, unconscionable, unfortunate delays . . ..

George McClellan's fabrications have survived and thrived for the past 150 years.

Burnside was besmirched; his betrayal was complete.

CHAPTER 33
Ground Truth

Stand upon the ground;
Listen to the ground speaketh.
—The author

PICTURE YOURSELF confronting a rattlesnake.

You're within striking distance of the angry reptile. It is coiled; its slanted eyes are glued to your every move, its forked tongue sensing, darting in and out between its sacs of poisonous venom; its mouth open, fangs exposed; its rattle shaking, warning you to stay away.

Oh, and this is not your ordinary rattler. It is wounded. You've been beating it with a shovel, trying to slice it into parts. The snake, smartly, has retreated, but now it's at the opening to its den, atop a high ridge. No more withdrawal. It will defend itself. The rattler recoils—and waits.

Your move.

I present this terrifying (for a coward like me) dilemma as an allegory depicting the situation on the day following the one-day Battle of Antietam. The rattlesnake is Robert E. Lee. George McClellan has been swinging the shovel. McClellan's attacks have forced Lee to abandon almost every position he held the previous morning, places like The Cornfield, the East Woods, the West Woods, the Dunker Church, Mumma Ridge, Bloody Lane and Burnside Bridge.

Though compelled to withdraw, Lee did not depart. He pulled back, taking a stand at even stronger positions on a higher, more compact elevation—a north-south ridgeline about 1,000 yards west of his previous deployments. Here he compressed his veteran fighters—atop the high ground—supported by nearly 250 cannon, massed and menacing, ready to kill at a distance. Here Lee waited on September 18, on high alert—and with high anxiety.

General McClellan could see Lee. Lee wanted to be seen. About one mile separated the fighting titans, both quiet, for the moment. The ground between them, however, was not quiet. Nearly 20,000 wounded soldiers cried for help, screaming in pain, begging for water, all crippled, many crawling, prostrate portions of human beings desperately searching for their lines. General Lee didn't say this here, but he probably was thinking what he later said: "It is well that war is so terrible, lest we grow too fond of it."[202]

Little Mac, too, witnessed his own injured army. Of every five U.S. soldiers in combat at Antietam, one had been smashed with bullets or shells—a shocking casualty rate.[203] For an average Northern family, that equated to one empty chair at the dinner table. McClellan, himself, seemed staggered. "The battle . . . without doubt, was the most severe ever fought on this continent," the general wrote to his wife Mary Ellen. "[F]ew more desperate were ever fought anywhere."[204]

But now posed the question—should McClellan renew the attack?

We discover McClellan's thinking, unlocked in two sentences to his wife: "The general result was in our favor; that is to say we gained a great deal of ground and held it. It was a success, but whether a decided victory depends upon what occurs today."[205]

That was at 8 a.m. on September 18th. Twelve hours later, after nary a shot fired by either side, General Lee retreated, under cover of darkness, back into Virginia. The wounded rattler returned to the protection of its den.

"Our victory was complete," McClellan telegraphed Washington the next morning. "The enemy was driven back into Virginia. Maryland and Pennsylvania are now safe."[206]

Half the country (Democrats) hailed McClellan for this achievement. The other half (Republicans) condemned him for permitting the wounded snake to escape. Political persuasion determined perspective. Both believed themselves correct in their point of view. "People do not seem to realize that their opinion (my emphasis) of the world," observed Ralph Waldo Emerson, "is also a confession of character." [207]

Antietam historians, for the most part, have unified around an opinion that the opportunity to attack and destroy Lee on September 18 was McClellan's greatest failure. I, myself, espoused this religion for four decades. The sermon sounded like this: if only McClellan possessed moral courage, he could have ended the war, then and there.

The historians' firm of Palfrey, Murfin & Sears greatly influenced my thinking. Civil War veteran Francis Palfrey explained the non-attack with persistent refrains. "[T]here was in McClellan a sort of incapacity of doing anything till an ideal completeness of preparation was reached." He was appalled, but not surprised by McClellan's consistency of ineptitude. "He did not use his own troops with sufficient promptness, thoroughness and vigor, to achieve great and decisive results." Palfrey then morphed into a psychologist: "The fault was in the man."[208]

James Murfin piled on during the Civil War centennial. "[H]e failed his army by not pursuing Lee . . . this must forever remain McClellan's folly." But Murfin preferred a contemporary hornet's sting, quoting a Chicago newspaper editor (Republican) soon after the battle: "What devil is it that prevents the [Northern] Army from advancing on the Rebels? . . . If it is McClellan, does not the President see that he is a traitor, and is plunging the nation into the gulf of destruction."[209]

Two decades following Murfin, Stephen Sears further powered these perceptions. McClellan "shrank from his paramount responsibility—to command. Repeatedly his men fought desperately to the threshold of victory, and repeatedly he let that victory slip away . . . in no instance did he honor that indisputable military maxim to reinforce success." When McClellan failed to attack on the 18th, Sears concluded he "remained in character, so fearful of losing that he could not risk winning."[210]

One salient factor is absent from each of these judgments—the ground where Lee stood.

Battles are not simply decisions of the mind. Battles, more typically, are decisions gone awry—altered by the vagaries of the ground. The ground (or terrain) can determine a decision; dupe a decision; delay a decision; detour a decision; and worst of all, destroy a decision. Every infantryman or infantrywoman who has engaged in warrior combat knows that—regardless of the best conceived plan, the ground dictates outcome.

No battlefield is two-dimensional. No book by any author, and no map by any cartographer, can replicate the ground of a battlefield. No words (no matter how many) can describe the battleground. Unlike a book or a map—with flat, soft, shiny surfaces produced by a printer—a battlefield displays hardened and distinctive geologic features, molded by the earth. Those molds "mold" a battle. The battleground is three-dimensional chess at its deadliest.

Speaking of three-dimensional chess, visualize Mr. Spock and Captain Kirk playing the game on the starship Enterprise. The "board" is vertical; not flat. The "pieces" are in multiple layers, suspended on rotating arms, attached to a central column. The pieces can be moved up (like ascending bluffs or slopes) or down (like descending into depressions or chasms)—equivalent to moving troops upon uneven ground.

Virtually every written study on Antietam ignores the importance of the ground. Understandable. Ground is not intended to be written, but walked.

To properly understand what an army commander is thinking, one must understand the ground. The first thing a Civil War general viewed and assessed, upon arrival at a potential battle site, was terrain. A series of questions would be asked: Where's the highest point?; how steep are the approaches?; is the cover wooded or open?; does the terrain undulate (wave up and down), or is it mostly flat?; where are blinds where the enemy can hide?; is the surface solid or swampy?; are there streams we need to cross?; is the enemy's position anchored, both on the right and left of its line, on a strong physical feature (such as high ground or a river)?; is my position anchored to prevent flanking?

Ultimately, the most important question was this: Is this ground most suitable for offense or defense? Or is it not suitable at all, so let's get out of here?

These queries only can be answered with an inspection of the ground. It's the first thing a military historian should do on any battlefield anywhere. Instead, we do it backward—we allow the after-action reports and narratives to form our opinions first. And for most Civil War narrative historians, they stop there. They don't "ground-truth" the narratives.

"Ground-truthing" is equivalent to yoga for a discerning Civil War historian. You stand upon the battlefield, close your eyes and clear your mind of everything you know about that battle. Then you open your eyes and then ask yourself the questions above. You do this over and again—walking (you can't do this from your car window)—slowly and studiously—to key points on the field. If you've succeeded in erasing from your brain the polluting post-battle punditry, you see a whole new picture, an entirely different landscape.

You now view the battlefield before it became a field of battle.

Congratulations! You have accomplished something few Civil War historians have mastered. Nothing—no written word, no colorful map, no gruesome photo of dead soldiers—time-transports you closer to the moment of conflict than standing upon the ground.

As I tell my groups, when leading battlefield tours: This is the power of place. Here is where your soles, through your inner-soul, connect with their souls.

So, returning to General McClellan and the question at hand—should he have attacked Lee on September 18th?

Had he done so, I predict his men would have been slaughtered. How do I know so? I've walked the ground.

Lee had positioned his Confederates on a high, north-south ridge—the highest between himself and the U.S. army. The vertical bluff rose more than one hundred feet in a steep incline, forming a natural fortress. More than one-half mile of open ground lay in front—ideal for pummeling, concentrated, converging artillery fire. Infantry could be sheltered, even hidden, on the back slope of this ridge, protecting soldiers from Yankee incoming; but more importantly, preventing the Federals from seeing troop concentrations and their locations. Lee also had the advantage of shifting troops rapidly behind the ridge, completely invisible to his enemy.

Still want to attack the wounded rattler?

A frontal assault against the Hauser's Ridge/Reel Ridge/Sharpsburg Ridge/Harpers Ferry Road ridgeline had prospects for disaster, not breakthrough.

McClellan could see this. He was on the ground. He knew what was before him. Had McClellan attacked Lee's September 18 position with a frontal assault, "McClellan's Charge" likely would have ended in a disaster for the Union army, regardless of McClellan's numeric advantage.

In terms best understood by Civil War aficionados, Lee's line at Sharpsburg was equivalent to the Union line at Cemetery Ridge at Gettysburg—the point of the famous Pickett's Charge.

We all know how that turned out for General Lee.

CHAPTER 34
Did McClellan Outthink Lee? Part III

The greater the interest involved in a truth
the more careful, self-distrustful, and patient
should be the inquiry.
—Harriett Beecher Stowe[211]

HUMAN KIND HAS EVOLVED into two types of beings.
Leaders and followers.

Few of us are leaders; most of us are followers. This is not a critique. I am not commending the leader, nor am I condemning the follower. Both, in fact, are dependent upon one another. Neither can exist without the other. If you, as the leader, have no followers, then you exist in a vacuum with no one to lead. If you, as the follower, have no leader, then you wander, aimless and empty and lost.

In truth, within each of us live both beings. They coexist, in suspension, until we call upon either the leader or the follower to emerge. We determine which being emerges depending upon our circumstances.

Two circumstances controlled General Lee and General McClellan following the Battle of Antietam—risk or quit.

Risk, by definition, is hazardous. Risk-taking is inherent in leadership. Assumption of risk requires consideration of multiple outcomes (many of them bad); confidence in your abilities to control outcomes (often not the case); and courage to implement (based upon faith, not certainty). Risk emboldens leaders. It frightens followers.

Quitting, or removing yourself from a circumstance, can be an act of courage or an act of cowardice. A leader knows when to quit; a follower just quits. The follower gives up, says it's too much, and runs from responsibility. The leader, before quitting, first reviews all risks remaining.

Historians have assessed the risk and quit for the day following the Battle of Antietam. They have concluded: 1. Lee chose risk (the courageous decision); and 2. McClellan selected to quit (the cowardly decision).

"What manner of man was he," observed the preeminent Lee biographer Douglas Southall Freeman, "who would elect after that doubtful battle against vast odds to stand for another day with his back to the river?"[212]

Dr. Freeman, and virtually every student of Antietam, has been awed by Lee's fortitude. But the moment was very matter-of-fact for Robert E. Lee: "We awaited without apprehension the renewal of the attack."[213]

Historians have fixated on the risk of Lee standing, outnumbered at least two-to-one, and concluded that his stance welcomed annihilation and the end of the greatest army in the Confederacy. That his risk literally risked the future of the Confederacy, and that the Southern dream of independence would die, forever, on Sharpsburg Ridge. "What manner of man was he . . .?"

Drama! We love drama. But we also have been trapped by adulation. Historians, once again, have failed us. And I've wandered among this crowd, a happy follower. Our job as historians is not to follow the conventional, but to challenge, as leaders, the accepted. Leaders inquire; followers perspire.

General Lee did take risk, but it was prudent risk—calculated, considered and controlled. He knew the odds. Two to one against him was just another day in the office. Lee faced those odds routinely throughout the war. Those advantages were not exclusive to General McClellan. It required four additional Union commanders after Antietam (and two-and-a-half more years of war) before U.S. Grant finally beat Lee with odds.

General Lee, additionally, owned the advantage of ground. He knew his reconstituted position on September 18 was the strongest position of defense he had occupied thus far in the war. He knew that high ground almost always could even out, and in many instances, defeat the odds. Lee's three-mile line was compact, connected and coordinated—and most important, deadly.

Lee dared McClellan to attack him. Was McClellan a coward for not attacking?

Here historians take a joy ride. Stephen Sears summarized best the historians' quintessential opinion of McClellan. "Since the first months of the war he had predicted for himself the command in one great decisive battle that would go far toward ending the Rebellion; when he finally came face to face with that reality, he was unable to recognize it." Sears concluded that McClellan "lost his inner composure and with it the courage to command under the press of combat."[214]

I have a question for all Antietam historians: Would you storm Sharpsburg Ridge (assuming you even know where it is)? Your answer not only will test your courage, but also your honesty.

The absent, but significant, story is this: McClellan refused to swallow Lee's bait.

Instead, simply by engaging in a stare down with Lee all day on September 18, McClellan won the will of wits. With barely firing a shot, and nearly without losing a soldier, McClellan forced Lee to retreat. Is that not a worthy accomplishment? Not only to retreat, but to abandon Maryland, leave the North, and cease the invasion. Are these not trophies of accomplishment?

General McClellan, you'll recall, five days earlier on the discovery of Special Orders 191, promised President Lincoln: "Will send you trophies."[215]

Yet historians have awarded McClellan no trophies. A principal reason was McClellan himself. In typical McClellan fashion, in an attempt to defend himself, he became his own worst enemy.

Instead of admitting the strength of Lee's position—and an almost guaranteed certainty that a frontal assault would result in a bloody and unparalleled repulse of the Union army—McClellan offered a pile of ( ) . . . excuses.

His troops were "greatly overcome by fatigue and exhaustion" (so were Lee's). They had faced "long day and night marches to which they had been subjected during the previous three days" (identical to Lee). His supply trains "were in the rear, and many of his troops had suffered from hunger" (ditto for Lee). His men had been "driven back in great disorder, and much scattered" (true as well for Lee before redeploying). Much of his artillery "had consumed all their ammunition . . . and it was impossible to resupply them" (a serious problem for Lee, too). "Finally, re-enforcements . . . had not arrived" (no re-enforcements were out there at all for General Lee).[216]

Eleven months after Antietam, after sustaining nearly a year of brutal attacks against his character for not destroying the Rebels, McClellan offered these excuses as his self-defense in his August, 1863, official report.

Every excuse distracted from the reality—Lee held a strong position, and McClellan was wise not to attack it. Little Mac should have stated this fact, and shut up. McClellan should have credited himself for not seizing Lee's bait, rather than giving his critics more ammunition to use against him.

In essence, McClellan forced Lee to quit—and McClellan possessed the self-discipline to quit himself. He recognized the imprudence of striking at Lee when Lee held the best hand (high ground). In other words, McClellan refused the temptation to chase a mirage, and as a result he chased General Lee away.

But Lee's "quit" was momentary. His withdrawal from Antietam acknowledged he could do nothing more there, other than defend himself. But defense was not in Lee's constitution; his forte was offense. Lee determined the Battle of Antietam would not be his final play.

Despite the browbeating McClellan had unleashed against the Confederate commander on battle day, and despite the bruises his army had suffered, Lee decided to renew the invasion. Antietam was just a brief delay, an unwanted diversion.

The withdrawal from Sharpsburg thus became a prelude to another attempt to invade the North—immediately! No pause, no rest, no time to desist. The Rebels must continue to resist.

So Lee developed a new strategy in the rapidly evolving chess match. He would cross the Potomac under cover of darkness, return into Virginia via a ford below Shepherdstown (in what is now West Virginia), then race northward toward Williamsport, Maryland. He would re-cross the river there, and continue the invasion in Yankeedom.[217]

Stop! Let's pause for a moment. Hadn't General Lee had enough?

No. Despite the bloodbath at Antietam, Lee still sensed opportunity. McClellan, indeed, had blocked his most direct route north, via the Sharpsburg-Hagerstown Turnpike. But an avenue of invasion still existed, and Lee knew it. It followed, in fact, his original line of supply from the Potomac to Hagerstown and into Pennsylvania. If Lee could conduct his own flanking march, establish a bridgehead at Williamsport, and outrace McClellan to Hagerstown, good reason existed for another attempt at invasion.

Perhaps Dr. Freeman's psychological query—"What manner of man was he?"—was more apt for Lee's daring renewed offensive rather than his stand at Sharpsburg on the defensive.

To accomplish this bold maneuver required three things: First, a secure passage at Williamsport, and second, men able to march nineteen miles hard and fast to beat the enemy to Williamsport. And third, a lackadaisical response from McClellan.

Objective No. 1 was accomplished easily. Lee sent Stuart's cavalry, and Stuart himself, to swiftly seize the river passage at Williamsport and to take control of the town. Done. Accomplished on September 19.

But then the plan backfired. McClellan anticipated Lee's move! And McClellan moved faster.

Little Mac sensed the new risk. He wasted no time in reacting to Lee's continued aggressiveness. The Federal commander first responded to the threat at Williamsport by rushing two brigades of U.S. cavalry toward the town. He then bolstered his initial response with three divisions of infantry and supporting cannon. In a flash, 18,000 Union soldiers descended upon the river town. General Stuart, recognizing a good time to quit, promptly abandoned the position on the night of September 20.[218] Yet again, McClellan had thwarted Lee's plans.

And once again, McClellan became his own worst enemy. Instead of highlighting this success, he reverted to typical McClellan, explaining in his official campaign report all the reasons (excuses) he could not advance or attack rather than extolling his accomplishments.

The result—Little Mac's masterful maneuver at Williamsport is lost in history. Due to the unexpected and aggressive response of McClellan, Lee's new offensive ended abruptly, less than 36 hours after it began. The Confederate commander expressed disappointment to his president, Jefferson Davis: "It was my intention to re-cross the Potomac," wrote Lee; to renew the invasion, "but the condition of the army prevented it."[219]

Interesting. Not a word from General Lee about McClellan blocking him. Not a single word in his correspondence with his boss, President Davis, about the enemy foiling his plan at Williamsport. Not one hint that McClellan had blocked his renewed offensive made it into Lee's official report of the campaign.

And historians have followed accordingly. Most have attentively, and dutifully, repeated Lee's excuse for quitting: His army no longer could "exhibit its former temper and condition. . . . I am, therefore, led to pause."[220]

Almost no one gives George McClellan credit as the principal cause for the pause.

CHAPTER 35
Still Photo

Preserve your memories,
keep them well,
what you forget
you can never retell.
—Louisa May Alcott[221]

ONE OF ANTIETAM'S GREATEST MYSTERIES surrounds a photo.

How can that be?

Nothing stirs memory more than a photo.

Photographs time-freeze a moment. A picture, literally, stops time. It captures an image—of an instant—in life. Photos enable us to relive a personal experience, whether it be a Christmas past with your favorite gift, or visits with grandparents, now perhaps passed. The selfie with friends allows us to remember ourselves in moments of social bonding or on a lifetime vacation experience.

What would we be—and where would we be—without photographs?

People who lived during the Civil War were the first generation of humans to live with photographs.

Prior to the advent of the first popularized form of photography (the "daguerreotype," unveiled in France in 1839), few people knew what other people looked like outside of their small social circles. Only the wealthy could afford painted portraits; and with

Lincoln and McClellan meeting at McClellan's headquarters at the Showman "Home Farm" south of Sharpsburg, October 3, 1862. Note the captured Confederate battle flag in the lower left, and the shadows, indicating the photo is taken in mid-morning as the sun rises over Showman's Knoll.
Courtesy of the Library of Congress.

the exception of an occasional sketch, we could never know how distant people appeared.

This explains why, if you're exploring genealogy, you cannot discover photographs of your ancestors. In my case, a photographic image beyond my great-great-great grandparents is impossible.

Even with the popularization of photography by the time of the Civil War, the process of taking a picture was complex, time-consuming and even hazardous because of the volatile and deadly chemicals used by the photographer. Film did not exist yet (and it's practically extinct today), and most photos were a negative image produced on a piece of glass. Cameras were heavy and cumbersome and so weighty that every camera required a tripod. For a photographer who carried his show on the road, a portable darkroom (usually a converted horse-drawn wagon) was essential.

No household or factory or studio had electricity, so the process depended exclusively on natural light, sometimes enhanced with mirrors. It was impossible to shoot a photograph at night, and almost as problematic to photograph anything moving—it became nothing but a blur.

Speaking of moving, we've all seen photos of Victorians, posing for portraits, looking stiff and stoic, never smiling, appearing in a perpetual state of shock. It's not because these people were robotic; but instead, when posing for a photo, they had to sit or stand—perfectly still—for seconds and seconds. Any movement, including an eye-blink, could foul up a photo.

I know this from personal trial and error, posing throughout my career for living history Civil War photographers. My favorite experience, however, was the day I married my wife Sylvia. Our official wedding photographer was the renowned Rob Gibson of Gettysburg, who used an original camera that had photographed Confederate president Jefferson Davis and other Civil War luminaries. We had to pose, absolutely still, for seconds—then it required Rob another twelve to fifteen minutes to produce one wet-plate glass negative. Sounds tedious, but it wasn't. We incorporated the photography into a post-ceremony interpretive demonstration that enthralled our guests. Today we proudly display the images as framed wall mounts in our Victorian parlor.

You'll never find, incidentally, an original Civil War-era photograph in color. Didn't exist. Well, bright colors did, but not the process to reproduce those colors in a photo. Tinted or hand-colored photos became popular, but that involved additional painting added to the glass image.

One more limitation on Civil War photography—a photo could not be mass-reproduced in a newspaper or a magazine. That process had not yet been defined, so photos appeared as illustrations, made from woodcuts, a highly refined form of artistry that enabled facsimile reproductions.

These printing limitations also prevented circulation of "Wanted" images in ubiquitous American post offices. Abolitionist John Brown, as example, wanted by the U.S. government for crimes committed before the Civil War in Bleeding Kansas, could live

A view of the famous Lincoln-McClellan meeting at the Showman
"Home Farm," October 3, 1862. This is the image that provided the hint
for the springhouse.
Courtesy of the Library of Congress.

without fear of recognition in the region of Harpers Ferry (or anywhere) because no one knew what he looked like.

By the time of the Civil War, entrepreneurs (professional photographers) had established studios throughout the country, ranging from major metropolitan areas like New York to rural farm
communities like Hagerstown and Frederick in Maryland. To "have
your likeness taken" often required an entire day of commitment,
traveling via horse-drawn carriage into town and back, dressed
in your Sunday best. A photo session cost a dollar or more, the
equivalent of one full day's wage for the average American worker.

The most famous photographer in the United States during the
Civil War was Matthew Brady. Renowned for his portrait studios
in New York City and Washington, D.C., possession of a "Brady"
was a badge of honor for socialites and politicians of their day.

Numerous famous photos of Abraham Lincoln were Brady's work, produced at his capital studio, along with images that the U.S. Treasury later replicated on the $5 bill and the Lincoln penny.

And now we transition . . .

"The Dead of Antietam" changed photography forever. The images became a national sensation. Dead men in the Bloody Lane; bloated bodies by the Burnside Bridge; corpses near The Cornfield; decomposing carcasses before the Dunker Church. Graphic gruesome and grotesque, people never before had seen war portrayed so realistically.

We cannot relate to the 1860s person who witnessed these graphic images. We, of course, are used to images of death and destruction and horror. In our world, our media flood us with imagery of the worst disasters and the worst of humanity—continuously. We see it so much that we almost become insensitive to the pain and suffering and devastation. It's so pervasive, it's no longer persuasive; it's not even unique.

But "The Dead of Antietam" shocked people. For the first time in American history, people saw—through a photographic exhibition—American soldiers dead on an American battlefield. "We recognize the battle-field as a reality, but it stands as a remote one ... It is like a funeral next door," observed a reporter with the *New York Times*, as he gazed at the gallery of dead. "It attracts your attention, but does not enlist your sympathy. But it is very different when the hearse stops at your own door, and the corpse is carried out over your own threshold."

Brady had achieved something revolutionary. He had dispatched two of his best photographers to Antietam (Alexander Gardner and James F. Gibson). They arrived too late for the battle, but in time to witness Union soldiers burying Confederate dead. Over several days, the two photographed nearly 90 pictures of unknown Confederate corpses, strewn over key landmarks on the Antietam landscape.

When the images appeared in Brady's Broadway gallery, thousands lined up to witness the spectacle. Displayed so boldly and so graphically in Mr. Brady's studio about one month after Antietam, the *New York Times* reporter was fascinated with this new realism of death. "Those who lose friends in battle know what battle-fields are," he mused. "[O]ur Marylanders, with their door-yards strewed with the dead and dying, and their houses turned into hospitals for the wounded, know what battle-fields are."

"Mr. BRADY has done something to bring home to us the terrible reality and earnestness of war," the reporter concluded. "If he has not brought bodies and laid them in our dooryards and along the streets, he has done something very like it."[222]

"The Dead of Antietam" offered me my first lesson in history—as detective work. About 115 years after the original New York City exhibition, while I was a sophomore at Shepherd College, historian William Frassanito resurrected the Antietam series. He published many photos in his novel and award-winning book *Antietam: The Photographic Legacy of America's Bloodiest Day.* But Bill did not simply reprint pictures. He used his talents as a former U.S. Army intelligence analyst, along with his passion for history and photography, to determine where the photos were taken on the battlefield—documenting the location of each shot and then matching it with a modern-day view.

Bill Frassanito transformed my impression of the Antietam landscape. He accomplished this by overlaying photos of the dead upon the landscape of today. The first time I truly time-tripped was through Bill's book, as he brought me right to September, 1862, and right to the camera location on the battlefield. Later on, some of my most thrilling memories as a tour guide were co-hosting Antietam tours with Frassanito—watching the audience stare in fascination at the ground—seeing nothing today, but recreating from yesterday the depictions of the dead. Bill had resurrected the dead (on the landscape) through the enduring power of the photograph.

Nearly forty years have passed since Bill first taught me his investigative techniques. But Bill's innovations helped lead me to my own discoveries—and solving the mystery of a famous Antietam photo.

Let me explain.

I live on a farm south of the Antietam Battlefield, and about two miles south of Burnside Bridge. My home, in fact, served as General Burnside's headquarters in the weeks following the battle. My

wife Sylvia and I lovingly and attentively have restored our home to its Civil War era appearance.

Two weeks following the battle, during the opening days of October, Abraham Lincoln arrived to congratulate his victorious army and to examine the Antietam Battlefield. En route he briefly visited with Burnside in our home, then proceeded to General McClellan's headquarters, where Lincoln and McClellan met to determine the future course of the war. None knew where this meeting occurred until recently.

Then I stumbled across something while researching in the National Archives.

I was examining a war claim for damages filed on behalf of the Civil War-era owner of my farm, Raleigh Showman. An amazing document, it described, down to the last fence rail, losses incurred as a result of the post-battle occupation of the house and farm by the Union army. Absolute devastation was caused by unwillingly hosting 10,000 men in a mini-city for two weeks on the Showman farm.

But within the war claim, I discovered information not only about my farm, but also about Raleigh's parents' farm, called the Home Farm—a beautiful stone house located about three-quarters mile north of my place.

The claim specifically identified the Home Farm as the site of McClellan's post-Antietam headquarters. It also indicated that the U.S. Signal Corps had destroyed a segment of woods on mountain land associated with the Home Farm property.

These fortunate and unexpected discoveries led, in turn, to what I believe are the locations of several famous Civil War photographs—taken on the Home Farm during President Lincoln's visit to Antietam. The photographer was Alexander Gardner.

One shows the president and General McClellan meeting inside his headquarters tent. This photo has been reproduced hundreds of times and viewed in television documentaries, magazines and countless books. But it's an interior view only. How can we associate this with the Showman's Home Farm?

An excellent clue is that the photo was taken at McClellan's headquarters. We've established that location at the Home Farm.

Further proof is provided by an exterior view—but not from a famous photograph. Instead, it's from an obscure image obtained by historian and writer Bob Zeller. In his excellent book, *Antietam in 3-D*, Bob and his co-authors present Antietam photographs in an entirely different way. In their book, published for the Civil War sesquicentennial (150th anniversary), the photos come vividly alive through 3-D glasses. This is no trick. Many of the original photos were designed to be viewed as three-dimensional images. The book even includes 3-D glasses to help the reader grasp the full breadth of these images.

One illustration reveals Lincoln and McClellan standing outside the headquarters tent, with landscape clearly visible in the background. Landscape background was a principal technique utilized by Frassanito—match something in the original photo with something on the modern landscape.

I was able to do that. In the background of the exterior tent photo appeared a tiny structure. At first glance, it looked like a small tent aligned with other tents; but with careful and magnified inspection, it definitely stood out as a small structure.

When comparing the photo with today's landscape, the small structure is visible. It still stands today! It is the original stone springhouse for the Home Farm.

Speaking of landscape, other Gardner photographs taken at the same time featured people at headquarters other than Lincoln and McClellan. These photos further confirmed background landscape features.

One example is Showman's Knoll, or the rounded peak jutting up behind the stone house on the Home Farm, that appeared in other illustrations. The elevation and accessibility to Showman's Knoll made it an ideal location for McClellan's headquarters signal station from the end of September through the first week of October. You'll recall President Lincoln visited in early October, accompanied by photographer Gardner.

The famous Gardner signal station photo—featuring the distinctive log-crib architecture—usually has been identified as atop Red Hill or Elk Ridge. The Army did have signal posts at both locations, one at Red Hill during the Battle of Antietam, and another

Signal station on Showman's Knoll.
Courtesy of the Library of Congress.

on Elk Ridge at Maryland Heights after the Federals reoccupied Harpers Ferry.

But those sites were not this station. Why would Gardner travel out of his way to those locations when he had a signal station within easy range immediately behind McClellan's headquarters?

Inspection today of the crest of Showman's Knoll reveals the original outline of the signal station—an entrenched square barely detectable within an 18th-century charcoal hearth (a flattened area where charcoal was produced as fuel for a nearby iron furnace). It also reveals the ruins of stone huts, laid out in company streets—the remains of the temporary homes of the signalmen. And as further evidence, while leading a tour for Antietam's licensed guides to this site, which is on private property, we literally kicked up from the ground a fully intact axe head that dated to the Civil War. We know, because we matched it up immediately by doing research on a smart phone.

Photographs spur memories. But what happens if everyone who can remember where the photos were taken is dead? The location of the photos passes away as well.

These famous Antietam photos, taken at McClellan's headquarters, document a heralded past.

For the first time, we now can associate their locations with the present.

And all along, the locations were within sight of my home.

CHAPTER 36
Temptation

Outward judgment often fails;
inward judgment never.
—Theodore Parker[223]

THE MOST POWERFUL PERSON in the United States is the president.

But not after Antietam.

Abraham Lincoln did not save the country from the Confederate invasion. George McClellan had accomplished that feat. The president had not protected Pennsylvania from the Rebels. General McClellan had earned that achievement. Lincoln had not organized a disorganized army, restored morale for demoralized soldiers, nor won victories on two battlefields on Northern soil. Those marvels belonged to McClellan.

"You should see my soldiers now!" the general wrote to his wife Mary Ellen three days after Antietam. Victorious and beaming with confidence, McClellan prided his army, almost as a personal possession. "You never saw anything like their enthusiasm—it surpasses anything you ever imagined."

McClellan had created this army, built and trained this army, defended this army, and now led this army to victory. His men praised him and adored him. McClellan recognized the adulation, accepted it, even thrived on it. "I don't believe that Napoleon even ever possessed the love and confidence of his men more fully that I do of mine," he wrote.[224]

His army, in fact, conferred McClellan his power. And because of his army, McClellan now was the most powerful man in America.

And a troubled man.

McClellan's victory at Antietam had produced an unwitting and unwelcome outcome for the general—emancipation.

Five days following the battle, President Lincoln used McClellan's triumph to trumpet a new destiny for the nation. The president determined the moment had arrived to initiate the end of slavery. Lincoln's Preliminary Emancipation Proclamation dramatically altered the course of the war. No longer was salvation of the Union the sole mission; henceforth, the war would have a dual purpose—reunion of the states and the eradication of slavery.

McClellan was horrified.

Had the president usurped his constitutional authority? Had Abraham Lincoln become a despot?

"The [President's] late Proclamation . . . render[s] it almost impossible for me to retain my commission & self respect at the same time," an angry and shaken McClellan expressed to his wife. "I cannot make up my mind to fight for such an accursed doctrine as that of a servile insurrection—it is too infamous."[225]

McClellan didn't simply disagree with Lincoln. This turn of events scorched his very being.

General McClellan adamantly rejected Lincoln's action. He viewed it as unnecessary at best, unprincipled and unconstitutional at worst. Had Lincoln become the resurrection of John Brown?

McClellan's political affinity with the doctrine of conservative Democrats aggravated his conscience. He diametrically opposed the Republican Party's political philosophy regarding slavery. Republicans supporting emancipation were not just wrong, they were evil.

McClellan had attempted to persuade Lincoln not to adopt such radical policy. Three months before Antietam, the Congress—absent most Southerners, who had seceded—was debating a law entitled "The Confiscation Act." The draft law permitted the United States to seize and confiscate property of Rebels, including slaves.

This legislation, led by Radical Republicans, greatly concerned McClellan. He pondered difficult questions, and was troubled by the direction of the government. Was property confiscation a legitimate power of the national legislature? What clause in the Constitution permitted confiscation of property? What legal instrument allowed the government to seize slaves?

Hoping Lincoln would intercede to control his Republican legislators, McClellan expressed his views in a multi-page letter to the president. "Military power should not be allowed to interfere with the relations of servitude, either by supporting or impairing the authority of the master," McClellan opined. "Neither confiscation of property . . . or forcible abolition of slavery should be contemplated for a moment."

Then McClellan concluded with a threat. "A declaration of radical views, especially upon slavery, will rapidly disintegrate our present Armies."[226]

McClellan's fellow Democrats were disturbed and distressed by what they considered extremism. So much so, in fact, that McClellan confided to his wife in early July: "I have commenced receiving letters from the North urging me to march on Washington & assume the Govt!!"[227]

Three months later, following Antietam, the president himself had become ensnared in the Radical Republican dream of emancipation. What should McClellan do?

His best friend, his military confidant, and his most loyal general was measuring the pulse. "The proclamation was ridiculed in the Army," revealed Fitz-John Porter, "caus[ing] disgust, dissident, and expressions of disloyalty to the views of the administration, and amount, I have heard, to insubordination."[228]

McClellan not only heard objection from within the ranks, but also from an aroused Northern populace. "The atmosphere around us is tremulous with changes; the air is full of revolution," recorded a New York newspaper correspondent. "He [the soldier] was willing to fight and die for the restoration of the Union, but not for the emancipation of the negro. He was against a war for this object."[229]

The *New York Herald* (a Democratic newspaper) minced no words. Emancipation "will go far towards producing an expression on the [Army] that will startle the country and give us a military dictator."[230]

Had the time arrived?—the moment for McClellan to march upon Washington?

Halt! Consider what we're considering. An army commander seizing power, overthrowing the president; ignoring the Congress; excusing the Supreme Court; and establishing and enforcing martial law through the power of the military. Nothing could be more un-American. This is impossible in America.

But yes—this was possible.

Never in the history of the United States was the nation ever so close to collapse of democracy and replacement with dictatorship. I am not hyperbolizing. Nothing but George McClellan could stop a takeover by George McClellan. The destiny of the United States, at this moment, belonged to George McClellan.

"I am very anxious," McCllelan wrote to a wealthy New Yorker and powerful Democratic operative," to know how you and men like you regard the recent Proclamation . . . inaugurating servile war, emancipating the slaves, & at one stroke of the pen changing our free institutions into a despotism."[231] McClellan was seeking counsel.

The temptation of power is great; the temptation to resist absolute power is near irresistible.

As McClellan ruminated on his options and the fate of his country the last week of September, he received word at his headquarters at the Showman family's Home Farm south of Sharpsburg that an important visitor would soon arrive—President Lincoln.

"The Pres[ident] was very kind personally," he shared with his wife following Lincoln's three-day visit. "[T]old me he was convinced I was the best general in the country . . . He was very affable & I really think he does feel very kindly toward me personally."[232]

Three days following Lincoln's departure, McClellan issued, from his Home Farm headquarters, "General Order No. 163."[233]

"Armed forces are raised and supported simply to sustain the civil authorities; and are to be held in strict subordination thereto in all respects. This fundamental rule of our political system is essential to the security of our [r]epublican institutions, and should be thoroughly understood and observed by every soldier."

Then McClellan concluded with the most American response. "The remedy for political errors ... is to be found only in the action of the people at the polls."

The most important order of General McClellan's life—was not on a battlefield.

McClellan, himself, had won his most important battle.

CHAPTER 37
Cows' Tails Mystery Resolved

*Are right and wrong convertible terms,
dependent upon popular opinion?*
—William Lloyd Garrison[234]

SOMEONE DESERVED the blame.

Somebody must pay the price for the disaster.

It's in our culture. It's who we are. The loser we must condemn.

The biggest loser in the Antietam campaign was Robert E. Lee. Let's examine his objectives. He failed to turn the people of Maryland in his favor; he failed to invade Pennsylvania and threaten any major Northern city; he failed to sway enough voters for Democrats to dethrone the Republican majority; he failed to persuade the English and French to support the Confederate cause; and—perhaps most important—he failed to defeat the U.S. army on Union soil.

The consequences for Lee: lost momentum, lost opportunities, and ultimately, a lost cause.

But history, instead of branding Lee the loser, has anointed George McClellan with the title.

McClellan, indeed, possessed despicable character traits, and we do love to hate him. But based on accomplishments during those first three weeks of September 1862—crucial days for the salvation of the nation—McClellan's performance is commendable. Little Mac ensured the protection of Washington; maneuvered to defend Baltimore; forced Lee to retire from the Pennsylvania front; handed Lee his first defeat at the Battle of South Mountain; compelled Lee into his first retreat to Sharpsburg; defeated Lee at Antietam; cornered Lee into a retreat back into Virginia; and guaranteed the end of the invasion at Williamsport.

Why, then, is McClellan the loser?

Because politics dictated he must be.

The most famous man in the United States following Antietam was George McClellan. The most successful general in the nation (by popular perception) following the defeat of the invasion was General McClellan. And the greatest political threat to President Lincoln and the continuance of Republican power—George Brinton McClellan. A Democrat.

Americans had a propensity for electing heroic generals as president. We started, of course, with George Washington. We followed with Andrew Jackson, hero of the Battle of New Orleans in the War of 1812. Then came William Henry Harrison, the conqueror at Tippecanoe. And then old Zachary Taylor of Mexican War renown, soon followed by Franklin Pierce, who also garnered a Mexican War star. In the 25 years preceding the Civil War, five of the nine presidents had been generals.

What if McClellan became the Democratic candidate opposing Lincoln in the presidential election (1864) two years hence?

Intolerable.

Partisan politics is an American tradition. We decry it, but we try it at every opportunity. Our founders did not wish this, and the Father of our Country warned us to avoid it. But something within our original 13-colony British genes compels us to call out and shout down our political adversaries. The more ludicrous the insult, the more thrilling our response. It's our longest and most endearing national sport.

So in the tradition of American politics, McClellan (a Democrat) became a target of the Republicans. McClellan's battlefield victories could not go unchallenged; he must be besmirched. His popularity must be diminished, his reputation sullied. His ascendancy into the White House must be stopped and his name tarnished. Republicans must conduct a war (within the Civil War) to defeat General McClellan.

Now what's the best target to sink McClellan's rising boat? Harpers Ferry!

The biggest blemish on McClellan's record (other than the refrain that he didn't destroy Lee's Army) was Harpers Ferry. The surrender of the U.S. garrison there had been a source of sore embarrassment for the Lincoln Administration. Even though the victory at Antietam had been a news flash, the continuing and nagging story in newsprint for weeks was the debacle at Harpers Ferry. How did that happen, the editors wondered. Who was responsible for the disaster? Someone must be held accountable. Someone must pay!

The Lincoln Administration, in response to this chorus of demands, established a military commission to investigate. Now that's the American Way.

Lincoln appointed as head of the commission a staunch and unabashed, boisterous and brash, friend and ally—Major General David Hunter. Hunter possessed all the features of a Republican henchman. His very appearance suggested a rough decorum and penchant for bullying. Vacant of guilt and shallow on conscience, Hunter was the ideal assassin of McClellan.

The military commission offered pretext for Hunter's (and the Republicans') foregone conclusions. But the pretext must be convincing. Subsequently, hearings began on October 4, conveniently on the same day Lincoln was departing from McClellan's camp and concluding his visit to Antietam. Fifteen full days of testimony occurred over the next four weeks, in closed session. Though the internal proceedings were secret, the press sniffed daily for any leaks.

Hunter's commission asked nearly 1,800 questions of 44 witnesses, ranging in rank from lieutenant to Major General Henry Halleck. It delved into the causes for the surrender, inquiring about defenses, deployments and commanders' decisions. It collected 900 pages of evidence—written in longhand, and still extant at the National Archives. It drew conclusions and issued opinions, especially concerning garrison commander Dixon Miles, who had died from a shell explosion at the end of the battle.

"An officer who cannot appear before any earthly tribunal to answer or explain charges gravely affecting his character is entitled to the tenderest care and most careful investigation," reported the commission.

Regardless of this sympathy, the commission concluded: "Colonel Miles's incapacity, amounting to almost imbecility, led to the shameful surrender of this important post."[235]

I can write an entire book on why this conclusion is "fake news" (perhaps I will!). Look elsewhere in this volume for refutation of Miles's reputation. But in typical scapegoat fashion, the commission gave no credit for the facts that Miles: 1. stood off Stonewall Jackson for three days; 2. did this without support and in total isolation; 3. held on despite being outnumbered two to one; 4. played against Stonewall's veterans with raw troops; 5. had the unanimous support of his brigade commanders for surrender, believing that "further resistance was not only useless, but would be a criminal waste of life"; and 6. his last orders were to hold Harpers Ferry "until the last extremity." None of this mattered in the commission's view. Miles was easy to blame.[236]

But Miles was not the target. He was a sideshow compared to the primary object of condemnation.

McClellan was the principal culprit.

To ensure McClellan's guilt, the commission called upon General Halleck to testify. Little Mac considered "Old Brains" Halleck a mortal enemy, and Halleck believed McClellan a fraud. Both men detested each other, and their hostilities were well known in Washington. So, in essence, the commission called upon Halleck as a witness hostile to hostile witness - McClellan.

How do I know? Let's examine the question posed to Halleck, presented here in its entirety:

"Will you state to the court at what time General McClellan was ordered to advance and repel the enemy invading the State of Maryland; at what time he did actually advance; the average number of miles marched by him per day in pursuit of the invading enemy, and if, in your opinion, General McClellan should have relieved and protected Harpers Ferry?"[237]

Re-read that—slowly.

Note the connotation—McClellan was slow in starting; slow in advancing; slow in pursuing; slow in repelling; and slow in relieving. Lincoln once suggested that McClellan suffered from a bad

case of "the slows." This query confirmed that notion. It intentionally was designed to prove McClellan's incapacity.

Halleck happily confirmed the preconceived outcome:

"I am of the opinion that it was possible for General McClellan
to have relieved and protected Harpers Ferry, and that he should
have done so."[238]

Of course so.

This hatchet response had an interesting irony—Halleck had
refused McClellan's request to remove the garrison from Harpers
Ferry before it was surrounded. Halleck, more so than anyone,
was responsible for the Federals holding the position. Not a word
about that, however, before the commission.

McClellan did not know about Halleck's testimony, nor was Mc-
Clellan invited to offer his own account of the Harpers Ferry disaster. That did not suit the political prescription.

On Monday, November 3, 1862, the commission issued its report. Quite a coincidence—the day before Election Day.

The commission "cannot, from any motives of delicacy, refrain
from censuring those in high command when it thinks such censure deserved." It then charged this: McClellan "could, and should,
have relieved and protected Harpers Ferry." As an exclamation, in
its final sentence, the commission explained, "Had the garrison
been slower to surrender or [McClellan's] army swifter to march,
the enemy would have been forced to raise the siege or have been
taken in detail."[239]

Let the political fallout commence.

The irony, of course, is that McClellan's victory at Antietam—his
conquest of Lee's invasion—bolstered, in many respects, the Republican Party.

Consider the political chaos for Lincoln and his friends had the
Confederates marched into Pennsylvania. They did not, because
McClellan stopped them. Think, for a moment, of extreme election losses for the Republicans in the upcoming fall plebiscite if
Lee was running around unfettered in U.S. territory. Didn't happen, because McClellan blocked the Rebels. Pause and ruminate
on Republican loss of control of the U.S. House and the possible
discontinuance of the war with the Democrats in charge. McClellan's September victories virtually guaranteed otherwise. And

what of emancipation? Without McClellan's triumph at Antietam, how would Lincoln and the Radical Republicans have dealt with emancipation?

The Republicans despised McClellan, but his successful actions in September 1862 salvaged the Republicans' future.

The irony for McClellan—his grandest achievement—ensured his demise.[240]

And speaking of demise, what about the cows' tails order?

Recall the perfunctory order that Colonel Miles sent to his commander on Maryland Heights during the Battle of Harpers Ferry. The order to hold the high ground at all hazards "until the cows' tails drop off." The order, that if followed, could have changed the direction of the campaign and altered American history.

The commission made a startling discovery.[241]

Turns out the "order" itself was never issued. It was "made up" to cover for a dead man. The order, itself, was a fraud.

Hmm—a recurring theme in history.

APPENDIX 1
Special Orders 191

SPECIAL ORDERS,   HDQRS. ARMY OF NORTHERN VIRGINIA
  No. 191   September 9, 1862

I. The citizens of Fredericktown being unwilling, while overrun by members of this army, to open their stores, in order to give them confidence, and to secure to officers and men purchasing supplies for benefit of this command, all officers and men of this army are strictly prohibited from visiting Fredericktown except on business, in which cases they will bear evidence of this in writing from division commanders. The provost-marshal in Fredericktown will see that his guard rigidly enforces this order.

II. Major Taylor will proceed to Leesburg, Va., and arrange for transportation of the sick and those unable to walk to Winchester, securing the transportation of the country for this purpose. Then route between this and Culpeper Court-House east of the mountains being unsafe will no longer be traveled. Those on the way to this army already across the river will move up promptly; all others will proceed to Winchester collectively and under command of officers, at which point, being the general depot of this army, its movements will be known and instructions given by commanding officer regulating further movements.

III. The army will resume its march to-morrow, taking the Hagerstown road. General Jackson's command will form the advance, and, after passing Middletown, with such portion as he may select, take the route toward Sharpsburg, cross the Potomac at the most convenient point, and by Friday morning take possession of the Baltimore and Ohio Railroad, capture such of them as may be at Martinsburg, and intercept such as may attempt to escape from Harpers Ferry.

IV. General Longstreet's command will pursue the same road as far as Boonsborough, where it will halt, with reserve, supply, and baggage trains of the army.

V. General McLaws, with his own division and that of General R. H. Anderson, will follow General Longstreet. On reaching Middletown will take the route to Harpers Ferry, and by Friday morning possess himself of the Maryland Heights and endeavor to capture the enemy at Harpers Ferry and vicinity.

VI. General Walker, with his division, after accomplishing the object in which he is now engaged, will cross the Potomac at Cheek's Ford, ascend its right bank to Lovettsville (sic), take possession of Loudoun Heights, if practicable, by Friday morning, Key's Ford on his left, and the road between the end of the mountain and the Potomac on his right. He will, as far as practicable, co-operate with Generals McLaws and Jackson, and intercept retreat of the enemy.

VII. General D. H. Hill's division will form the rear guard of the army, pursuing the road taken by the main body. The reserve artillery, ordnance, and supply trains, &c., will precede General Hill.

VIII. General Stuart will detach a squadron of cavalry to accompany the commands of Generals Longstreet, Jackson, and McLaws, and, with the main body of the cavalry, will cover the route of the army, bringing up all stragglers that may have been left behind.

IX. The commands of General Jackson, McLaws, and Walker, after accomplishing the objects for which they have been detached, will join the main body of the army at Boonsborough or Hagerstown.

X. Each regiment on the march will habitually carry the axes in the regimental ordnance-wagons, for use of the men at their encampments, to procure wood &.

By command of General R. E. Lee
R. H. CHILTON, *Assistant Adjutant-General*

APPENDIX 2
Lee's Proclamation to the People of Maryland

HEADQUARTERS ARMY OF NORTHERN VIRGINIA
Near Fredericktown, MD., September 8, 1862

To the People of Maryland:

It is right that you should know the purpose that brought the army under my command within the limits of your State, so far as that purpose concerns yourselves. The people of the Confederate States have long watched with the deepest sympathy the wrongs and outrages that have been inflicted upon the citizens of a commonwealth, allied to the States of the South by the strongest social, political, and commercial ties. They have seen with profound indignation their sister State deprived of every right and reduced to the condition of a conquered province. Under the pretense of supporting the Constitution, but in violation of its most valuable provisions, your citizens have been arrested and imprisoned upon no charge and contrary to all forms of law. The faithful and manly protest against this outrage made by the venerable and illustrious Marylander, to whom in better days no citizen appealed for right in vain, was treated with scorn and contempt; the government of your chief city has been usurped by armed strangers; your legis-

209

lature has been dissolved by the unlawful arrest of its members; freedom of the press and of speech has been suppressed; words have been declared offenses by an arbitrary decree of the Federal Executive, and citizens ordered to be tried by a military commission for what they may dare to speak. Believing that the people of Maryland possessed a spirit too lofty to submit to such a government, the people of the South have long wished to aid you in throwing off this foreign yoke, to enable you again to enjoy the inalienable right of freemen, and restore independence and sovereignty to your State. In obedience to this wish, our army has come among you, and is prepared to assist you with the power of its arms in regaining the rights of which you have been despoiled.

This, citizens of Maryland, is our mission, so far as you are concerned. No constraint upon your free will is intended; no intimidation will be allowed within the limits of this army, at least. Marylanders shall once more enjoy their ancient freedom of thought and speech. We know no enemies among you, and will protect all, of every opinion. It is for you to decide your destiny freely and without constraint. This army will respect your choice, whatever it may be; and while the Southern people will rejoice to welcome you to your natural position among them, they will only welcome you when you come of your own free will.

R. E. LEE
General, Commanding

APPENDIX 3
General Orders No. 163

HEADQUARTERS ARMY OF THE POTOMAC
October 7, 1862 – 11:35 p.m.

THE PRESIDENT OF THE UNITED STATES:
I have issued the following order, on your proclamation:
GENERAL ORDERS No. 163

HEADQUARTERS ARMY OF THE POTOMAC
Camp near Sharpsburg, Md., October 7, 1862

The attention of the officers and soldiers of the Army of the Potomac is called to General Orders, No. 139, War Department, September 24, 1862, publishing to the army the President's proclamation of September 22.

A proclamation of such grave moment to the nation, officially communicated to the army, affords to the general commanding an opportunity of defining specifically to the officers and soldiers under his command the relation borne by all persons in the military service of the United States toward the civil authorities of the Government.

The Constitution confides to the civil authorities—legislative, judicial, and executive— the power and duty of making, expounding, and executing the Federal laws, Armed forces are raised and

211

supported simply to sustain the civil authorities, and are to be held in strict subordination thereto in all respects. This fundamental rule of our political system is essential to the security of our republican institutions, and should be thoroughly understood and observed by every soldier. The principle upon which, and the object for which, armies shall be employed in suppressing Rebellion, must be determined and declared by the civil authorities, and the Chief Executive, who is charged with the administration of the national affairs, is the proper and only source through which the needs and orders of the Government can be made known to the armies of the nation.

Discussions by officers and soldiers concerning public measures determined upon and declared by the Government, when carried at all beyond temperate and respectful expressions of opinion, tend greatly to impair and destroy the discipline and efficiency of troops, by substituting the spirit of political faction for that firm, steady, and earnest support of the authority of the Government which is the highest duty of the American soldier. The remedy for political errors, if any are committed, is to be found only in the action of the people at the polls.

In thus calling the attention of this army to the true relation between the soldier and the Government, the general commanding merely adverts to an evil against which it has been thought advisable during our whole history to guard the armies of the Republic, and is so doing he will not be considered by any right-minded person as casting any reflection upon that loyalty and good conduct which has been so fully illustrated upon so many battle-fields.

In carrying out all measures of public policy, this army will, of course, be guided by the same rules of mercy and Christianity that have ever controlled its conduct toward the defenseless.

By command of Major-General McClellan:

JAS. A. HARDIE
Lieutenant-Colonel, Aide-de-Camp, and
Acting Assistant Adjutant-General

Notes

CHAPTER 1

[1] Napoleon's quote is from http://www.azquotes.com/author/1621-Napoleon_Bonaparte. Each chapter begins with a quotation from a writer or philosopher contemporary to the Civil War era. I used www.azquotes.com as my source for opening chapter quotes throughout the book. Individual quotations are located within the listing. Other online sources recommended for quotations include www.brainyquote.com and www.goodreads.com.

[2] Emerson's quote is from *Essays*, "History," (1841) https://archive.vcu.edu/english/engweb/transcendentalism/authors/emerson/essays/history.html

[3] Emerson, from *Essays*, "History," https://archive.vcu.edu/english/engweb/transcendentalism/authors/emerson/essays/history.html

[4] Emerson, from *Essays*, "History," https://archive.vcu.edu/english/engweb/transcendentalism/authors/emerson/essays/history.html

CHAPTER 3

[5] Hawthorne's quote is from http://www.azquotes.com/author/6414-Nathaniel_Hawthorne

[6] Lincoln presented his "House Divided Speech" at the Illinois State Capitol in Springfield on June 16, 1858, when accepting the

Republican nomination for U.S. Senate. Lincoln's quote is from http://www.abrahamlincolnonline.org/lincoln/speeches/house.htm

[7] Calhoun's quote appears in an article in *Civil War Times* by Ethan Rafus and is from http://www.historynet.com/john-c-calhoun-he-started-the-civil-war.htm

[8] Calhoun's quotes are from http://www.azquotes.com/author/2341-John_C_Calhoun

[9] Supreme Court's Dred Scott excerpt (1857) is from http://www.digitalhistory.uh.edu/disp_textbook.cfm?smtID=3&psid=293

[10] Lincoln delivered his "Speech on the Dred Scott Decision" in Springfield, Ill. on June 26, 1857. Excerpts from http://www.virginia.edu/woodson/courses/aas-hius366a/lincoln.html

CHAPTER 4
[11] Melville quote is from http://www.azquotes.com/author/9959-Herman_Melville

CHAPTER 5
[12] Cooper's quote is from http://www.azquotes.com/author/3248-James_F_Cooper?p=3

[13] *New York Times* accolade for Freeman is from https://en.wikipedia.org/wiki/Douglas_Southall_Freeman

[14] Douglas Southall Freeman, *R.E. Lee: A Biography,* Vol. II (New York: Charles Scribner's Sons, 1934), 378, footnote 3.

[15] Thoreau's quote is from http://www.azquotes.com/author/14637-Henry_David_Thoreau

[16] W. H. Morgan, *Personal Reminiscences of the War of 1861-5: In Camp, En Bivouac, on the March, on Picket, on the Skirmish Line, on the Battlefield, and in Prison* (J.P. Bell, Lynchburg, VA: 1911), 141-142.

[17] Morgan, 138, 143.

[18] Morgan, 141-142.

NOTES

CHAPTER 6

[19] Louisa May Alcott quote is from http://www.azquotes.com/author/200-Louisa_May_Alcott

[20] For the full text of Special Orders 191, see Appendix 2.

[21] *The War of the Rebellion: A Compilation of the Official Records of the Union and Confederate Armies* (hereafter *OR*) Vol. 19, Pt. 2, 281. McClellan to Lincoln, September 13, 1862. McClellan's message to the president was as follows: "I have the whole Rebel force in front of me, but am confident, and no time shall be lost. I have a difficult task to perform, but with God's blessing will accomplish it. I think Lee has made a gross mistake, and that he will be severely punished for it. The army is in motion as rapidly as possible. I hope for a great success if the plans of the Rebels remain unchanged. We have possession of Catoctin [mountain at Braddock Gap]. I have all the plans of the Rebels, and will catch them in their own trap if my men are equal to the emergency. I now feel that I can count on them as of old. All forces of Pennsylvania should be placed to cooperate at Chambersburg. My respect to Mrs. Lincoln. Received most enthusiastically by the ladies [public demonstration of appreciation in Frederick]. Will send you trophies. All well, and with God's blessing will accomplish it."

[22] D. H. Hill's comment on the "Lost Order" or "Lost Dispatch" appears in a footnote in Hill's article, "The Battle of South Mountain, or Boonsboro," *Battles and Leaders of the Civil War, Vol. II* (New York: The Century Company, 1887), 570 (footnote). Hereafter cited as *Battles and Leaders*.

[23] Walter H. Taylor, *Four Years with General Lee*, (New York: D. Appleton & Co., 1878), 67.

CHAPTER 7

[24] Parker's quote is from http://www.azquotes.com/author/11329-Theodore_Parker

[25] George B. McClellan, *The Civil War Papers of George B. McClellan*, ed. Stephen W. Sears (New York: Tichnor and Fields, 1989), 348, 135, 374, 361, 363. Hereafter cited as *McClellan Papers*.

These quotations are from multiple letters McClellan wrote to his wife in July, 1862, but with one exception: McClellan's comment that he had lost regard and respect for the Administration as heartless villains was written to the owner of the *New York World*, a Democratic political operative newspaper.

26 Francis W. Palfrey, *The Antietam and Fredericksburg* (New York: Charles Scribner's Sons, 1882), 41, 22-23, 60, 127.

27 James V. Murfin, *The Gleam of Bayonets: The Battle of Antietam and Robert E. Lee's Maryland Campaign, September, 1862* (New York: A.S. Barnes & Co., 1964), 172, 9.

28 Stephen W. Sears, *Landscape Turned Red: The Battle of Antietam* (New York: Ticknor & Fields, 1983), 303, 310. Hereafter cited as Sears, *Landscape*. Stephen W. Sears, *George B. McClellan: The Young Napoleon* (New York: Ticknor & Fields, 1988), 322-323. Hereafter cited as Sears, *Young Napoleon*.

CHAPTER 8

29 Anthony quote is from http://www.azquotes.com/author/466-Susan_B_Anthony

30 *OR*, Vol. 19, Pt. 2, 600. Lee to Davis, September 8, 1862,

CHAPTER 9

31 Henry Ward Beecher quote is from http://www.azquotes.com/author/1130-Henry_Ward_Beecher

32 Dennis E. Frye, *September Suspense: Lincoln's Union in Peril* (Harpers Ferry, WV: Antietam Rest Publishing, 2012), 148. Hereafter cited as Frye, *September Suspense*.

33 *OR*, Vol. 19, Pt. 2, 590. Lee to Davis, September 3, 1862.

34 *OR*, Vol. 19, Pt. 2, 601-602. Lee's "Proclamation to the People of Maryland," issued at Frederick, September 8, 1862. See Appendix 3 to view entire proclamation.

35 Frye, *September Suspense*, 10-11.

36 Frye, *September Suspense*, 8.

CHAPTER 10

37 Whitman quote is from http://www.azquotes.com/author/15605-Walt_Whitman

[38] Following the U.S. defeat at the First Battle of Bull Run on July 21, 1861, President Lincoln became convinced that the war would not cease in a short period. Lincoln recognized that he required a more organized, disciplined and professional fighting force to quash the Southern Rebellion. Based on the recommendation of General Winfield Scott (equivalent today to the head of the Joint Chiefs of Staff), Lincoln promoted McClellan to coordinate all Union field armies, to prepare the defenses of Washington and to establish an army to operate against Confederates in the Virginia and Richmond sector. McClellan promptly created and trained the Army of the Potomac—the largest army to that point in American history. After McClellan methodically directed his army to within three miles of Richmond in the spring and early summer of 1862 (in what's been dubbed the Peninsular Campaign), General Lee launched a series of counterattacks at the end of June (the Seven Days Battles) that forced McClellan to retire from Richmond and assume a defensive position along the James River. These setbacks and McClellan's subsequent inaction frustrated Lincoln, resulting in the president stripping McClellan of his command responsibilities by late August, 1862.

[39] Salmon P. Chase, "Diary and Correspondence of Salmon P. Chase" in the *Annual Report of the American Historical Association, Vol. 2* (Washington, D.C.: Government Printing Office, 1902), 50.

[40] *McClellan Papers*, 428.

[41] *OR*, Vol. 19, Pt. 2, 208-209. B&O Railroad president John W. Garrett to Secretary of War Edwin M. Stanton, September 7, 1862.

[42] *OR*, Vol. 19, Pt. 2, 200. Brig. Gen. Alfred Pleasonton, Army of the Potomac chief of cavalry, to R. B. Marcy, McClellan's chief of staff, September 7, 1862. OR 19, Pt. 2, 207. Maj. Gen. John E. Wool, commanding from Baltimore, to President Lincoln, September 7, 1862. *OR*, Vol. 19, Pt. 2, 203. Pennsylvania Governor Andrew Curtin to John E. Wool, September 7, 1862.

[43] *OR*, Vol. 19, Pt. 2, 222. Marcy to Maj. Gen. Ambrose E. Burnside, commanding the Union I Corps and IX Corps of the Army of the Potomac, September 9, 1862, 10 p.m. *OR*, Vol. 19, Pt. 2, 211. Mc-

Clellan to General-in-Chief Henry W. Halleck, September 8, 1862, 8 p.m.

CHAPTER 11

44 Emerson's quote is from http://www.azquotes.com/author/4490-Ralph_Waldo_Emerson

45 Gideon Welles, *The Diary of Gideon Welles, Secretary of the Navy under Lincoln and Johnson* (New York: Houghton Mifflin Co., 1911)

46 Harpers Ferry, from the outset of the war, was a strategic location for both United States and Confederate States objectives. Located on the border between North and South, with only the Potomac River separating the two warring nations, the Ferry changed hands eight times and hosted five battles between 1861-1864. Harpers Ferry became a target less than 24 hours after Virginia's secession, when Virginia militia was ordered to seize the U.S. Armory and Arsenal at the Ferry. U.S. troops blew up the arsenal, but the Virginians seized the armory and later transported its machinery south to Richmond and Fayetteville, N.C., where it was used to manufacture weapons for the South. In the war's earliest days, General Lee first acknowledged its strategic location at the northeastern gateway into the Shenandoah Valley, ordering it defended, and assigning Thomas Jonathan Jackson his first command of the war at Harpers Ferry in April, 1861. Two months later, the Rebels abandoned the position, opening Harpers Ferry to occupation by U.S. forces. By the spring of 1862, the Federals were using the B&O Railroad as a supply depot from which to launch invasions into Confederate territory and the Shenandoah Valley.

47 *OR,* Vol. 19, Pt. 2, 594. Lee to Davis, September 5, 1862. OR 19, Pt. 2, 597. Lee to Davis, September 7, 1862.

48 *OR,* Vol. 19, Pt. 1, 757. Halleck to Colonel Dixon Miles, commanding at Harpers Ferry, September 7, 1862.

49 *OR,* Vol. 19, Pt. 1, 758. McClellan's telegram request to Halleck, September 11, 1862. *OR,* Vol. 19, Pt. 2, 254. McClellan's request in

a letter to Halleck to remove Harpers Ferry garrison, September 11, 1862.

[50] *OR*, Vol. 19, Pt. 1, 758. Halleck to McClellan, September 11, 1862.

CHAPTER 12

[51] Dickinson's quote is from http://www.azquotes.com/author/3956-Emily_Dickinson

[52] See Appendix 2 for the specifics of Special Orders 191.

[53] James Longstreet, "The Invasion of Maryland," *Battles & Leaders*, Vol. II, 663. General Lee had three principal subordinates in this campaign: Stonewall Jackson, James Longstreet and James Ewell Brown (J.E.B.) Stuart. Jackson was renowned for his aggressiveness; Longstreet revealed tendencies toward caution and defense. Stuart commanded the cavalry.

CHAPTER 13

[54] Harriett Beecher Stowe quote is from http://www.azquotes.com/author/14207-Harriet_Beecher_Stowe

[55] *OR*, Vol. 19, Pt. 1, 790. Wool to Miles, September 5, 1862, sent on the second day of the invasion. For a complete narrative on the Battle of Harpers Ferry, see: Dennis E. Frye, *History and Tour Guide of Stonewall Jackson's Battle of Harpers Ferry* (Harpers Ferry, WV: Harpers Ferry Historical Association, 2012). This is adapted from a feature article written by the author for *Blue and Gray Magazine* for its September 1987 issue—the 125th anniversary of the battle.

[56] The "Railroad Brigade" that Miles commanded was never a brigade. It actually equated to a U.S. division or corps, numbering between 6,000 and 15,000 men, or six to ten times the usual strength of a brigade. Although headquartered at Harpers Ferry, Miles's men patrolled 350 miles of railroad, stretching from just west of Baltimore to the South Branch of the Potomac River. Miles understood his mission was to protect the railroad and its bridges from Confederate guerrillas. He emphasized his force did not exist "with the intention of fighting an army."

[57] Miles eventually deployed about 4,000 men to defend Maryland Heights. He stationed nearly 8,000 on Bolivar Heights. Nobody was placed on Loudoun Heights.

[58] Maryland Heights soars to 1,463 feet above sea level at its pinnacle, about 1,200 feet above the town of Harpers Ferry. Maryland Heights is about 300 feet taller than Loudoun Heights and about 800 feet higher than Bolivar Heights.

[59] *OR*, Vol. 19, Pt. 1, 852. From after-action report of Maj. Gen. Lafayette McLaws, October 18, 1862. McLaws commanded four brigades within his own division (about 4,000 men), and was assigned command of Richard Anderson's division as well (an additional 4,000 men).

[60] *OR*, Vol. 19, Pt. 1, 863. From Brig. Gen. Joseph B. Kershaw's after-action report, September 25, 1862. Kershaw commanded a brigade of about 1,000 South Carolina troops.

[61] The largest regiment in the Union army at Harpers Ferry—the 126th New York Infantry, boasting nearly 1,100 men—defended the center of the breastworks. Eight of the regiment's ten companies were on the crest of the mountain. The 126th had been in the army for only 22 days, having been mustered into service on August 22, 1862. Though an inexperienced regiment, Miles anchored the 126th with more experienced men, placing on its right the 32nd Ohio and on its left the 39th New York. This line held for nearly four hours. At about 10:30 a.m., however, the colonel of the 126th (Eliakim Sherrill) fell with a shot in the jaw. The loss of their commander panicked some in the 126th, and the Union defense at the breastworks crumbled. Sherrill survived this wound, but would be killed in the Battle of Gettysburg on July 3, 1863.

[62] The brigade commander in charge of the defense of Maryland Heights was Colonel Thomas H. Ford of the 32nd Ohio Infantry. Of Miles's junior brigade officers, Ford had the most experience, but that was quite limited. In typical Civil War fashion, Ford had "earned" his command of the 32nd Ohio because he had served as a former lieutenant governor of the Buckeye State. Between

3 and 3:30 p.m., Ford ordered his force to retire from the mountain, believing his line had again broken. "You are hereby ordered to fall back to Harpers Ferry in good order. Be careful to do so in good order." (*OR*, Vol. 19, Pt. 1, 619). After the battle, Ford claimed that Miles gave him discretion to withdraw.

[63] *OR*, Vol. 19, Pt. 1, 537. The order appears in the report of Lt. Henry M. Binney, Miles's aide-de-camp, filed on September 18, 1862, only three days after the surrender. Colonel Miles submitted no report, as he was mortally wounded by an exploding artillery shell incoming from Loudoun Heights soon after the decision to surrender. Miles died on the 16th at his headquarters at the Master Armorer's House. This building still stands today and is part of Harpers Ferry National Historical Park. It was the author's residence for ten years from 1979-1989.

[64] *OR*, Vol. 19, Pt. 1, 576. This eye-witness account is from Rev. Sylvester W. Clemans, chaplain of the 115th New York Infantry, presented as testimony before the Harpers Ferry Military Commission, October 7, 1862.

CHAPTER 14

[65] Cooper quote is from http://www.azquotes.com/author/3248-James_F_Cooper?p=3

[66] You can still follow Jackson's route today. I suggest using a map to follow along with these directions. When departing Frederick, follow Alt. 40 to Middletown. You will cross the Catoctin Mountain at Braddock Heights (known as Braddock Gap during the war). You will cross South Mountain at Turner's Gap, and then to Boonsboro, where Jackson camped on the night of September 10. Proceed through Boonsboro, and then turn left onto Md. 68, toward Williamsport. You'll cross the Potomac on the U.S. 11 bridge, downstream from the ford Jackson used. Follow Rt. 11 into downtown Martinsburg and North Queen Street. Turn left onto E. Burke Street. This becomes Golf Course Road. Follow it as it becomes Van Clevesville Road. Once you depart Berkeley County, it becomes Warm Springs Road. Turn left onto Shenan-

doah Junction Road, then right onto Daniel Road. Then right onto Flowing Springs Road, and a quick left onto Country Club Road. This will bring us to U.S. 340. Turn left toward Harpers Ferry, and you will be paralleling the original turnpike that connected Harpers Ferry with Charles Town.

[67] Jackson's column was the last of the three to arrive, pulling up on School House Ridge (opposite Bolivar Heights and about one mile distant from School House Ridge) at 11 a.m. on the 13th. McLaws' column was the first to arrive, entering Pleasant Valley north of Harpers Ferry on the 12th, then ascending Maryland Heights on the night of the 12th-13th. John G. Walker's division of about 4,000 men captured Loudoun Heights soon after dawn on the 13th without firing a shot. Miles did not defend that position.

[68] *OR*, Vol. 19, Pt. 1, 790. These are the preemptory orders Miles received from his department commander in Baltimore, Gen. John E. Wool, on September 5, 1862.

[69] *OR*, Vol. 19, Pt. 1, 953. This quotation comes from Jackson's official battle report, dated April 23, 1863.

CHAPTER 15

[70] Bronson Alcott quote is from http://www.azquotes.com/author/198-Amos_Bronson_Alcott

[71] State Line is the name of the community today.

[72] *OR*, Vol. 19, Pt. 2, 592. Lee to Davis, September 4, 1862, on the first day of the invasion.

[73] Frye, *September Suspense*, 160.

[74] Frye, *September Suspense*, 156.

[75] *OR*, Vol. 19, Pt. 2, 606. Dispatch written to McLaws from A. L. Long, Lee's military secretary, from Hagerstown on September 13, 1862.

[76] *OR*, Vol. 19, Pt. 2, 607. Message sent to McLaws from T.M.R. Talcott, Lee's aide-de-camp at 10 p.m. on September 13. Location not stated, but probably sent from Hagerstown.

CHAPTER 16

[77] Higginson quote is from http://www.azquotes.com/author/20830-Thomas_Wentworth_Higginson

[78] The most accurate account of the discovery of the orders is found in a letter from Sgt. Bloss to his home in Indiana, written on September 25, 1862. The letter is unpublished. It was discovered, however, in the possession of Bloss descendants by Tracy Evans, NPS curator/ranger at Monocacy National Battlefield. Evans exhibited the original letter during the 150th anniversary (2012) of the campaign. The letter provided specifics on the location of the Lost Orders (by a locust tree in a wheat field); and it noted only two cigars rather than the customary three. Bloss stated that he "immediately took it to General Gordon, he said it was worth a Mint of Money & sent it to General McClellan."

[79] *OR*, Vol. 19, Pt. 2, 281. McClellan to Lincoln, September 13, 1862. McClellan time-dated his note to the president as noon.

[80] It is false to contend that McClellan made no moves on September 13 in response to his discovery of the Lost Orders. At 3 p.m., he shared the Lost Orders with cavalry commander Pleasonton and instructed him to ascertain the accuracy of the enemy positions (*OR*, Vol. 51, Pt. 1, 829). At 3:35 p.m., McClellan ordered two divisions of IX Corps (Cox and Rodman, totaling about 6,000 men), as part of Burnside's wing command, to begin marching west toward Middletown (*OR*, Vol. 51, Pt. 1, 827). McClellan also instructed all three divisions of Joseph Hooker's I Corps to commence moving from New Market west toward Frederick on the afternoon of the 13th (*OR*, Vol. 51, Pt. 1, 828).

[81] Sears , *Landscape*, 117.

[82] Sears, *Landscape*, 120.

[83] "Opinion can be so perverted . . ." is a James Fenimore Cooper quote from http://www.azquotes.com/author/3248-James_F_Cooper?p=3

[84] *OR*, Vol. 19, Pt. 1, 146. From Lee's official report, August 19, 1863.

[85] *OR*, Vol. 19, Pt. 1, 817. From Stuart's official report, February 13, 1864.

CHAPTER 17
[86] Mott quote is from http://www.azquotes.com/author/21588-Lucretia_Mott
[87] Palfrey, 22-23.
[88] Murfin, 161.
[89] Sears, *Landscape*, 120-121.
[90] Welles, 107.

CHAPTER 18
[91] Child quote is from http://www.azquotes.com/author/2813-Lydia_M_Child
[92] Douglas Southall Freeman, *Lee's Lieutenants: A Study in Command,* Vol. II (New York: Charles Scribner's Sons, 1943), 716-718. Hereafter cited as *Lee's Lieutenants*. Dr. Freeman copies verbatim two "highly interesting memoranda of conversations held on the same day, Feb. 15, 1868, with General Lee at Lexington." Lee at that time was serving as president of Washington College. One memoranda was by Colonel William Allan, who had served as a close aide of Lee's throughout the war, and was a professor at Washington College. The other memoranda came from E. C. Gordon, who was a clerk at Washington College. Both men spoke with Lee about the Lost Order on the same date in 1868. The two memoranda were handed down to the son of Colonel Allan, who sent them to Dr. Freeman. Freeman includes nine pages of discussion on Special Orders 191 in his only appendix in volume two.
[93] Freeman, *Lee's Lieutenants*, 718.
[94] Sears, *Landscape*, 113, 125.
[95] Murfin, 165.
[96] Freeman, *Lee's Lieutenants*, 721.
[97] *OR*, Vol. 19, Pt. 1, 140. Lee to Davis, September 16, 1862.
[98] *OR*, Vol. 19, Pt. 1, 814-821. Stuart's official campaign report, February 13, 1864.
[99] *OR*, Vol. 19, Pt. 1, 146. Statement in Lee's official campaign report, August 19, 1863.

[100] Dennis E. Frye, *Antietam Revealed: The Battle of Antietam and the Maryland Campaign as You have Never Seen it Before* (Collingswood, NJ: C.W. Historicals, LLC), 18.

[101] *OR*, Vol. 19, Pt. 1, 42-43. McClellan's official campaign report, August 4, 1863.

[102] *OR*, Vol. 19, Pt. 1, 146.

CHAPTER 19

[103] Henry Ward Beecher quote is from http://www.azquotes. com/author/1130-Henry_Ward_Beecher

[104] *OR*, Vol. 19, Pt. 2, 590. Lee to Davis, September 3, 1862.

[105] *OR*, Vol. 19, Pt. 2, 592. Lee to Davis, September 4, 1862.

[106] *OR*, Vol. 19, Pt. 2, 591. Lee to Davis, September 3, 1862.

[107] *OR*, Vol. 19, Pt. 2, 606. Lee to Davis, from Hagerstown, September 13, 1862.

[108] South Mountain is a north-south ridge that runs the entire length of Maryland. The Battle of South Mountain occurred on Sunday, September 14, and it involved fighting at four gaps. At each location Lee's Confederates were defending and McClellan's Federals attacking. Geographically, starting from the south is Crampton's Gap, six miles from Harpers Ferry. Six miles further north is Fox's Gap, where the fighting began soon after dawn and continued into the darkness. Fox's Gap was the bloodiest action at South Mountain. One mile further north was Turner's Gap, through which passed the National Road leading between Frederick and Boonsboro. Still one mile further north was the Frostown Gap (so-labeled by modern historians) that constituted the extreme left flank of Lee's position. At the end of the day, the only position the Confederates continued to hold in strength was Turner's Gap.

[109] *OR*, Vol. 19, Pt. 2, 289. McClellan to Halleck, September 14, 1862, 9:40 p.m. *OR*, Vol. 19, Pt. 2, 294. McClellan to Halleck, September 15, 1862, 8 a.m. *OR*, Vol. 19, Pt. 2, 295. Lincoln to Hon. J. K. DuBois, Springfield, Ill., September 15, 1862, 3p.m.

[110] *OR*, Vol. 19, Pt. 1, 147. Lee's official campaign report, August 19, 1863.

[111] *OR*, Vol. 19, Pt. 1, 140. Lee to Davis, September 16, 1862, from Sharpsburg.

[112] *OR*, Vol. 51, Pt. 2, 618-619. Lee to Lafayette McLaws, defending Pleasant Valley north of Harpers Ferry, September 14, 1862, 8 p.m.

CHAPTER 20

[113] Barton quote is from http://www.azquotes.com/author/998-Clara_Barton

[114] *OR*, Vol. 19, Pt. 2, 607. Jackson to McLaws, September 14, 1862, 7:20 a.m. No records indicate the death of any civilians during the bombardment. Most Federal positions were on the slopes of Bolivar Heights, so the town of Bolivar was spared possible destruction.

[115] *OR*, Vol. 19, Pt. 2, 607. Jackson to McLaws, September 14, 1862, 7:20 a.m.

[116] Dennis E. Frye, *Harpers Ferry Under Fire* (Harpers Ferry, WV: Harpers Ferry Historical Association), 88. Quotation of Lt. James H. Clark, 115th New York Infantry.

[117] Ambrose Powell (A. P.) Hill led his division on the successful flanking maneuver that seized the Chambers Farm on the extreme Union left on Bolivar Heights. Moving in the darkness of September 14-15, Hill overcame vertical bluffs and steep ravines to deploy more than 4,000 men as close as 150 yards to the enemy position. His artillery was within 1,000 yards of the U.S. lines and in position to enfilade the Federals' left and center (*OR*, Vol. 19, Pt. 1, 980). Today this battlefield ground is preserved as part of Harpers Ferry National Historical Park, thanks to the descendants of Alexander Murphy and the Trust for Public Lands.

[118] Frye, *Harpers Ferry Under Fire*, 93 (Clark quotation). Louis B. Hull, 60th Ohio Infantry, 89. Colonel Miles held a council of war with his brigade officers during this intense bombardment, and the decision to surrender was unanimous. Six reasons were given as cause for the surrender: 1) loss of Maryland Heights; 2) long-range ammunition expended; 3) no hope of reinforcement; 4) an enemy double the Federals' strength; 5) prevent sacrifice of

life "without a reasonable hope of success"; and 6) a unanimous decision that "further resistance was useless." (*OR*, Vol. 19, Pt. 1, 531).

[119] *OR*, Vol. 19, Pt. 1, 951. Jackson to Lee, September 15, 1862, near 8 a.m., from Harpers Ferry. The surrender of 12,737 soldiers was the largest capitulation of U.S. forces during the Civil War, and is second only to the fall of Bataan during World War II. Jackson also captured 73 cannon, 13,000 small arms, 200 wagons, and 1,200 army mules. (*OR*, Vol. 19, Pt. 1, 955, 549). The Confederate commissary reported seizing 155,954 pounds of hard bread, as well as 19,267 pounds of bacon and 4,930 pounds of coffee. My condolences to whoever counted this stuff. (*OR*, Vol. 19, Pt. 1, 961). It was the most lop-sided victory of the war for Jackson, as he suffered losses of only 39 killed and 247 wounded. Nearly 75 percent of the Confederate casualties occurred in the battle for Maryland Heights.

CHAPTER 21

[120] Harriett Beecher Stowe quote is from http://www.azquotes.com/author/14207-Harriet_Beecher_Stowe

[121] See Appendix 2 for specific instructions for McLaws in Special Orders 191.

[122] *OR*, Vol. 19, Pt. 2, 606. A.L. Long, Lee's military secretary, to McLaws, September 13, 1862, written from Hagerstown.

[123] *OR*, Vol. 51, Pt. 2, 618. Lee to McLaws, September 14, 1862, 8 p.m.

[124] *OR*, Vol. 19, Pt. 2, 608. R. H. Chilton, Lee's assistant adjutant general, to McLaws, September 14, 1862, 11:15 p.m.

[125] *OR*, Vol. 19, Pt. 1, 856. McLaws' official campaign report, October 18, 1862.

[126] *OR*, Vol. 19, Pt. 1, 856. McLaws' official campaign report, October 18, 1862.

[127] *OR*, Vol. 19, Pt. 1, 720. This quote appears in the testimony of Maj. Charles H. Russell, 1st Maryland Cavalry, before the Harpers Ferry Military Commission, October 16, 1862.

[128] The Confederates that the U.S. cavalry encountered at Sharpsburg were marching south from Hagerstown as part of General Lee's redeployment of the army on September 14. They were not Confederates retreating from South Mountain, who had not yet arrived at Sharpsburg. The wagon train at Williamsport was Longstreet's reserve ammunition train. It had moved from Hagerstown to Williamsport earlier on the 14th as part of Lee's redeployment, and was awaiting instructions. If Lee decided to remain in Maryland, the wagons were on his anticipated line of supply between Virginia, Maryland and Pennsylvania. If Lee determined to retreat back into Virginia, the train had use of an excellent ford at Williamsport. Reports on the number of wagons captured varied from as low as 40 to a high of 91. Frye, *Antietam Revealed*, 36-38.

[129] *OR*, Vol. 19, Pt. 1, 855. McLaws' official campaign report, October 18, 1862.

[130] *OR*, Vol. 19, Pt. 1, 47. Maj. Gen. William B. Franklin, commander of VI Corps, to McClellan, September 15, 1862, 11 a.m.

CHAPTER 22

[131] Hawthorne quote is from http://www.azquotes.com/author/6414-Nathaniel_Hawthorne

[132] *OR*, Vol. 19, Pt. 1, 45. McClellan to Franklin, September 13, 1862, 6:20 p.m. This is the order historians have fixated upon in condemning McClellan for his delayed response to the Lost Orders. McClellan had commenced moving the northern wing of his army, located near Frederick, on the afternoon of the 13th. Much of the Union IX Corps was across the Catoctin range by the evening of the 13th and located at Middletown, poised to advance against South Mountain on the 14th. See McClellan's report, *OR*, Vol. 19, Pt. 1, 48, for disposition of U.S. forces.

[133] Bronson Alcott quote is from http://www.azquotes.com/author/198-Amos_Bronson_Alcott

[134] The two gaps nearest Harpers Ferry were the South Mountain Potomac River gap, two miles east of the Ferry, and Crampton's Gap, six miles to the north. The two Confederate divisions op-

erating north of Harpers Ferry were Lafayette McLaws's and Richard Anderson's, totaling about 8,000 men. Based upon a numbers system that consistently overestimated Confederate strength, however, U.S. estimates would have placed this strength at 24,000. Based upon this assessment, Franklin is outnumbered two-to-one, giving reason for McClellan's desire to assist him.

[135] *OR*, Vol. 19, Pt. 1, 45. McClellan to Franklin, September 13, 1862, 6:20 p.m.

[136] *OR*, Vol. 19, Pt. 1, 47. Franklin to McClellan, September 14, 1862, 11 a.m.

CHAPTER 23

[137] Stanton quote is from http://www.azquotes.com/author/14012-Elizabeth_Cady_Stanton

[138] Dickens's quotes are from http://charlesdickenspage.com/america.html

[139] Freeman, *R.E. Lee*, Vol. I, 420-421.

[140] *OR*, Vol. 9, Pt. 1, 951. Jackson to Lee, September 14, 1862, 8:15 p.m.

CHAPTER 24

[141] Douglass quote is from http://www.azquotes.com/author/4104-Frederick_Douglass

[142] *OR,* Vol. 19, Pt. 2, 606. Lee to Davis, September 13, 1862, from Hagerstown.

[143] *OR,* Vol. 19, Pt. 2, 254. McClellan to Halleck, September 11, 1862, from Rockville.

[144] Confederate casualties equaled 35,774 from the end of June through early September, compiled from Confederate returns. OR 18, 751, shows field returns for the department protecting the Confederate capital, including Richmond, equaled 13,210 men on October 1.

[145] The source for Halleck's 150,000 was Chase, *Diary and Correspondence*, 58. *OR*, Vol. 19, Pt. 2, 248 revealed Pennsylvania Gov. Andrew Curtin estimating 200,000 in a September 10 message to McClellan.

[146] *OR*, Vol. 19, Pt. 2, 248. The clergyman's estimate of 120,000 appeared within Curtin's September 10 note to McClellan.

[147] *OR*, Vol. 19, Pt. 2, 254. McClellan to Halleck, September 11, 1862.

[148] McClellan, *McClellan Papers,* 310. McClellan to Secretary of War Edwin M. Stanton, June 25, 1862.

[149] Murfin, 127.

[150] Murfin, 48.

CHAPTER 25

[151] Bronson Alcott quote is from http://www.azquotes.com/author/198-Amos_Bronson_Alcott

CHAPTER 26

[152] Sojourner Truth quote is from http://www.azquotes.com/author/14828-Sojourner_Truth

[153] *OR*, Vol. 19, Pt. 2, 590. Lee to Davis, September 3, 1862.

[154] *OR*, Vol. 19, Pt. 2, 590. "(T)hrowing off the oppression" quote is from Lee to Davis, September 3, 1862. *OR*, Vol. 19, Pt. 2, 596, expresses Lee's disappointment of no general uprising by the people of Maryland. Lee to Davis, September 7, 1862, from Frederick.

[155] *OR,* Vol. 19, Pt. 2, 605. Lee to Davis, September 12, 1862, from Hagerstown.

[156] *OR*, Vol. 51, Pt. 2, 618-619. Lee to Lafayette McLaws, trapped in Pleasant Valley north of Harpers Ferry, September 14, 1862.

[157] *OR,* Vol. 19, Pt. 1, 140. Lee to Davis, September 16, 1862, from Sharpsburg.

[158] *OR,* Vol. 19, Pt. 1, 140. Lee to Davis, September 16, 1862, from Sharpsburg.

[159] *OR, Vol.* 51, Pt. 2, 618-619. Lee to McLaws, September 14, 1862.

[160] *OR,* Vol. 19, Pt. 2, 281 is source for "all the plans of the [R]ebels." *OR,* Vol. 19, Pt. 2, 294 is source for "perfect panic" and "shockingly whipped." McClellan to Halleck, September 15, 8 a.m.

OR, Vol. 19, Pt. 2, 294 is source for "rout and demoralization." McClellan to Halleck, September 15, 1862, 10 a.m.

CHAPTER 27
[161] Theodore Parker quote is from http://www.azquotes.com/author/11329-Theodore_Parker
[162] Palfrey, 60, 62.
[163] Palfrey, 49, 47.
[164] Murfin, 208, 327.
[165] Sears, *Landscape*, 163. Sears, *Little Napoleon*, 294.
[166] McClellan, *McClellan Papers*, 466. McClellan to Mary Ellen, September 16, 1862, 7 a.m.

CHAPTER 28
[167] Child quote is from http://www.azquotes.com/author/2813-Lydia_M_Child
[168] Sears, *Landscape*, 175.
[169] Murfin, 206.
[170] Sears, *Landscape*, 176.
[171] Palfrey, 60.
[172] Palfrey, 60.

CHAPTER 29
[173] Thoreau quote is from http://www.azquotes.com/author/14637-Henry_David_Thoreau
[174] Once McClellan determined that Lee intended to stay and stand on the 17th, the Federals attacked. Commencing at dawn, the Union I Corps of Joseph Hooker launched against the Confederate line held by Stonewall Jackson in The Cornfield and the East Woods. Those assaults were repulsed. But then the Union XII Corps arrived and outflanked the right of the Rebel position, forcing the Confederates to withdraw into the West Woods behind the Dunker Church. McClellan ordered the II Corps to reinforce and to continue the assault. Its momentum was thwarted with a vicious Confederate counterattack in the West Woods, led

by Lafayette McLaws's troops arriving from Harpers Ferry. Lee's left then stabilized.

The action then shifted south to Lee's right center (Bloody Lane) where the U.S. divisions of William French and Israel Richardson hammered the Alabama brigade of Robert Rodes and North Carolina brigade of George B. Anderson, both under the direction of D. H. Hill. Reinforcements arrived from Harpers Ferry under Richard Anderson, but to no avail, as the Federals eventually seized the Bloody Lane position by early afternoon.

Though breached here, Lee's men retired to higher ground along Hauser-Reel ridge and on Sharpsburg ridge, where the National Cemetery is today. In other words, Lee reformed his line on higher ground after he lost the Bloody Lane position.

Meanwhile, further to the south, the U.S. IX Corps was attacking the Burnside Bridge, taking it by 1 p.m. Burnside then followed by launching the largest attack of the day against the Confederate right, but this failed when A. P. Hill's division arrived from Harpers Ferry, blunting Burnside's assault. The battle ended at dusk. Lee remained the next day, redeployed on high ground west of his original position on the 17th. McClellan did not attack again on the 18th, and Lee withdrew across the Potomac that night.

[175] OR, Vol. 19, Pt. 1, 1024. Quote taken from Hill's official campaign report that is undated, other than to say "1862." Hill claimed that the "Yankees were now so demoralized that a single regiment of fresh men could drive the whole of them across the Antietam."

[176] OR, Vol. 19, Pt. 1, 840. The story is from Longstreet's official campaign report, filed on October 10, 1862.

[177] Edward Porter Alexander, *Military Memoirs of a Confederate* (New York: Charles Scribner's Sons, 1907), 262.

[178] Jacob Dolson Cox, "The Battle of Antietam," *Battle & Leaders,* Vol. II, 656 (footnote).

[179] Alexander, 242. Alexander explains his absence on this page. He states that he met General Lee at Sharpsburg on the 16th, and "was ordered to collect all empty wagons and go to Harpers Fer-

ry and take charge of the surrendered ammunition. . . I was soon on my way back [into Virginia], and encamped that night [the 16th-17th] with many wagons not far from Harpers Ferry."

[180] *Battles & Leaders,* Vol. II, 656. The basis for this quotation is a footnote to a lengthy article by Jacob D. Cox entitled "The Battle of Antietam." Cox is not the source of the quotation. It came from Thomas M. Anderson, who served with the 9th U.S. Infantry on Antietam battle day. Anderson was in reserve on the east bank of the creek, near the Union center. Anderson, himself, did not hear the conversation between McClellan and several officers. But he states that he learned of the quote through Gen. George Sykes, who was present at the McClellan meeting. In sum, the pedigree of this quotation is: 1) Fitz-John Porter said it; 2) Sykes heard it; 3) Anderson learned it from Sykes years after the war; and 4) Anderson repeated it and wrote about it in 1886. You determine its validity.

[181] William B. Franklin, "Notes on Crampton's Gap and Antietam," *Battles & Leaders,* Vol. II, 597.

[182] *OR,* Vol. 19, Pt. 1, 47. Franklin to McClellan, September 14, 1862, 11 a.m.

CHAPTER 30

[183] Emerson quote is from http://www.azquotes.com/author/4490-Ralph_Waldo_Emerson

[184] McClellan, *McClellan Papers,* 183. McClellan to his mother, February 16, 1862.

[185] McClellan, *McClellan Papers,* 382. McClellan to Mary Ellen, August 2, 1862.

[186] McClellan, *McClellan Papers,* 486. McClellan to Mary Ellen, September 29, 1862.

[187] McClellan, *McClellan Papers,* 374. McClellan to Mary Ellen, July 27, 1862.

[188] Maj. Gen. John Pope, commanding the Union army at the Battle of Second Bull Run/Second Manassas) was considered by McClellan—and hence Porter—as an arch enemy. Pope knew this, and he blamed Porter for delinquency in arriving at the battle-

field and delaying execution of orders. Pope felt so much animus against Porter that he blamed him for his defeat and charged him with treason.

[189] *OR*, Vol. 19, Pt. 2, 308. Message sent to Burnside from McClellan's aide-de-camp and acting assistant adjutant general. Curiously, no name is signed on the message.

[190] *OR*, Vol. 19, Pt. 2, 297. Special Orders (no number given) issued on September 15, 1862.

[191] *OR*, Vol. 19, Pt. 2, 314. This response was written on September 17 (battle day), but no time is given on the message.

[192] Murfin, 269. Sears, *Landscape*, 170-171.

CHAPTER 31

[193] Mark Twain, On the Decay of the Art of Lying, 1880. Quote is from http://www.online-literature.com/twain/1320/

[194] Twain quote is from http://www.online-literature.com/twain/1320/

[195] *OR*, Vol. 19, Pt. 1, 30. From McClellan's preliminary report of the battle, October 15, 1862.

CHAPTER 32

[196] Henry Ward Beecher quote is from http://www.azquotes.com/author/1130-Henry_Ward_Beecher

[197] McClellan, *McClellan Papers,* 469. McClellan to Mary Ellen, September 18, 1862, 8 a.m. Interesting that the general dashed this off to his wife while wearily awaiting events the morning after the battle.

[198] McClellan, *McClellan Papers,* 473. McClellan to Mary Ellen, September 20, 1862.

[199] Chase, 94. The diary entry is for September 25, 1862. Hooker was recuperating after being wounded in the lower leg/ankle area about 8:30 a.m. near the Dunker Church. Many were aware that the conniving Hooker was angling to replace McClellan as Army commander.

[200] *OR*, Vol. 19, Pt. 1, 914. This maneuver is confirmed in the re-

port of Brig. Gen. John G. Walker, who had been assigned on Lee's far right to protect against any crossing of the lower bridge and fords in that vicinity. "Soon after 9 a.m. [on the 17th], I received orders from General Lee . . . to hasten to the extreme left." Walker moved his entire division of about 3,600 Confederates—a maneuver impossible to miss from the U.S. signal station on nearby Red Hill.
201 *OR*, Vol. 19, Pt. 1, 63-64. Each of these quotes is extracted from McClellan's official campaign report, August 4, 1863.

CHAPTER 33
202 Freeman, *R. E. Lee*, Vol. II, 462. Lee supposedly made this statement to General Longstreet during the Battle of Fredericksburg on December 13, 1862—a smashing Confederate victory. Freeman writes, "Turning to Longstreet he revealed the whole man in a single brief sentence."
203 Murfin, 297. Murfin claims 55,956 U.S. soldiers available to fight on September 17. Total Federal casualties were 12,410 casualties, or a 21.8 percent loss.
204 McClellan, *McClellan Papers* 473. McClellan to Mary Ellen, September 20, 1862, 8 a.m.
205 McClellan, *McClellan Papers*, 469. McClellan to Mary Ellen, September 18, 8 a.m.
206 *OR*, Vol. 19, Pt. 2, 330. McClellan to Halleck, September 19, 1862, 10:30 a.m.
207 Emerson quote is from http://www.azquotes.com/author/4490-Ralph_Waldo_Emerson
208 Palfrey, 134, 127.
209 Murfin, 327, 300. The letter was written by Joseph Medill of the *Chicago Daily Tribune* to O. M. Hatch, Illinois secretary of state and a close friend of Lincoln's.
210 Sears, *Landscape*, 310, 303.

CHAPTER 34
211 Harriett Beecher Stowe quote is from http://www.azquotes.com/author/14207-Harriet_Beecher_Stowe

[212] Freeman, *R.E. Lee*, Vol. II, 404.

[213] *OR*, Vol. 19, Pt. 1, 151. From Lee's official campaign report, August 19, 1863.

[214] Sears, *Young Napoleon*, 322-323.

[215] *OR*, Vol. 19, Pt. 2, 281. McClellan's message to Lincoln announcing his discovery of the Lost Order, September 13, 1862.

[216] *OR*, Vol. 19, Pt. 1, 66-67. From McClellan's official report, August 4, 1863.

[217] *OR*, Vol. 19, Pt. 1, 142; *OR*, Vol.19, Pt. 2, 626-627. Lee presented his intentions to reignite the invasion in two messages to President Davis, the first on September 20 and the second on September 25.

[218] To inaugurate Lee's new offensive, J.E.B. Stuart crossed the Potomac at an obscure ford above Sharpsburg on the 18th, taking Wade Hampton's cavalry brigade with him. The cavalry marched all that night and re-crossed the Potomac above Williamsport at Mason's Ford on the 19th. Meanwhile, a part of the 12th Virginia Cavalry, along with a battalion of the 2nd Virginia Infantry (local men from the Lower Shenandoah Valley) had established a bridgehead at the town on the 19th. Stuart then moved his cavalry to commanding ridges overlooking the town, awaiting the arrival of the remainder of Lee's army.

McClellan responded with alacrity and force. He ordered two brigades of cavalry toward Williamsport, followed by 6,000 newly arrived and fresh reinforcements from Darius Couch's division. In support of the cavalry and Couch, McClellan then directed Franklin's VI Corps to Williamsport on the 21st. (*OR*, Vol. 19, Pt. 1, 68; Part 2, 334-335).

Lee's offensive toward Williamsport was arrested, not only because of McClellan's show of strength at that point, but also because the Federals had unexpectedly crossed the river at Boteler's Ford below Shepherdstown on September 19-20, threatening his rear. This compelled Lee to recall Jackson and A. P. Hill's division "to rectify occurrences in that quarter." (*OR*, Vol. 19, Pt. 1, 141).

[219] *OR*, Vol. 19, Pt. 2, 627. Lee to Davis, September 25, 1862.

[220] *OR*, Vol. 19, Pt. 2, 627. Lee to Davis, September 25, 1862.

CHAPTER 35

[221] Louisa May Alcott quote is from http://www.azquotes.com/author/200-Louisa_May_Alcott

[222] *New York Times* quotes—"Dead of Antietam"—are from http://www.nytimes.com/1862/10/20/archives/bradys-photographs-pictures-of-the-dead-at-antietam.html

CHAPTER 36

[223] Parker quote is from http://www.azquotes.com/author/11329-Theodore_Parker

[224] McClellan, *McClellan Papers,* 476. McClellan to Mary Ellen, September 20, 1862.

[225] McClellan, *McClellan Papers,* 481. McClellan to Mary Ellen, September 25, 1862.

[226] McClellan, *McClellan Papers*, 344-345. McClellan to Lincoln, July 7, 1862. The general hand-delivered this letter to the president during Lincoln's visit to Harrison's Landing on the James River.

[227] McClellan, *McClellan Papers* 351. McClellan to Mary Ellen, July 11, 1862.

[228] Sears, *Young Napoleon*, 325.

[229] *Philadelphia Inquirer*, "Our New York Letter," September 25, 1862, p. 8, col. 5.

[230] Sears, *Young Napoleon*, 325.

[231] McClellan, *McClellan Papers*, 482. McClellan to William H. Aspinwall, September 26, 1862. Aspinwall had made a fortune in shipping, was part of New York City's elite, and was a Democratic Party powerhouse. Aspinwall visited McClellan soon after Lincoln's departure and advised him to follow the directive of the commander in chief.

[232] McClellan,*McClellan Papers*, 489-490. McClellan to Mary Ellen, October 5, 1862.

[233] *OR*, Vol. 19, Pt. 2, 395-396. See Appendix 4 for entire text of General Orders No. 163.

CHAPTER 37

[234] Garrison quote is from http://www.azquotes.com/author/5367-William_Lloyd_Garrison

[235] *OR*, Vol. 19, Pt. 1, 799.

[236] *OR*, Vol. 19, Pt. 1, 776.

[237] *OR*, Vol. 19, Pt. 1, 786. The commission asked Halleck this question on the next to last day of testimony.

[238] *OR*, Vol. 19, Pt. 1, 787.

[239] *OR*, Vol. 19, Pt. 1, 800.

[240] The Democrats selected McClellan as their presidential nominee to run against Lincoln in the 1864 election. Whatever popularity he had gained with the public as a result of his defeat of Lee's invasion certainly did not translate into votes. Lincoln won the electoral college 212-21. The popular vote went for Lincoln 55 percent to 45 percent for McClellan. Lincoln carried all but two states. McClellan won only in Kentucky and his home state of New Jersey.

[241] *OR*, Vol. 19, Pt. 1, 79-780. The fraudulent order was uncovered by the defense team for Col. Thomas Ford, commander of the force upon Maryland Heights. The order was written following the surrender and after the death of Col. Miles by Lt. Henry M. Binney, Miles's aide-de-camp. Ford's defense team uncovered the hoax by examining the letter book of Miles and seeing the order not listed chronologically (i.e., inserted after the fact). This was the only order in the book out of order.

APPENDIX 1

[242] *OR*, Vol. 19, Pt. 2, 603-604.

APPENDIX 2

[243] *OR*, Vol. 19, Pt. 2, 601-602.

APPENDIX 3

[244] *OR*, Vol. 19, Pt. 2, 395-396.

My Top Forty

There was a day when every kid had a portable phonograph playing vinyl 45 rpm records based on a weekly Top Forty Countdown. It was a brilliant scheme to sell the hot commodities devised by some slick Manhattan marketing firm—so successful, in fact, that Top Forty Countdown is forever part of American culture from the mid-twentieth century.

Here's a take on this theme. Below I present "My Top Forty" books on Antietam and the first invasion of the North. I trust you'll find this much more interesting than the traditional bibliography.

My principal purpose in this book is to provoke you, spur your curiosity and to encourage you to seek answers to your questions. I also hope to make history fun, and permit your escape from dry, boring, esoteric exercises. To assist you with your exploration, "My Top Forty" offers you resources that will inspire your own further investigation. I've organized by subject categories that appear throughout the main text. These will help you organize your own research. I've added, as well, my own brief notation about each book. I've designed this as a practical guide to help you locate a book that interests you. I do include the standard information on author, title and publication; but other than that, this looks very different from your traditional bibliography.

Oh, and by the way, a disclaimer—with the exception of the first category, I know most of the authors. Many have been friends for decades, and I respect and admire their research and their writings. That does not mean, however, that I agree with their findings. So, be tantalized, and explore for yourself My Top Forty.

SOURCES THAT BRING YOU CLOSEST
TO THE STORY AS IT'S HAPPENING

Chase, Salmon P. "Diary and Correspondence of Salmon P. Chase," *Annual Report of the American Historical Association, Vol. 2.* Washington, D.C.: Government Printing Office, 1902. Lincoln's Secretary of Treasury shares remarkable and unfettered insights on Lincoln, McClellan and the turmoil of the first weeks of September, 1862.

Frye, Dennis E. *September Suspense: Lincoln's Union in Peril.* Antietam Rest Publishing: Harpers Ferry, WV, 2012. I love Civil War newspapers, and this book tells the story of the participants in their own words through period papers. I spent two years researching newspapers North and South to present the history as it was happening, and to bring readers as close as possible to what people in 1862 were understanding and feeling as events were unfolding. My goal was to immerse you in the action as it occurred.

Hay, John. *Inside Lincoln's White House: The Complete Civil War Diary of John Hay.* Ed. Michael Burlingame and John R. Turner Ettlinger. Southern Illinois University Press: Carbondale and Edwardville, IL,1997. Hay was Lincoln's assistant presidential secretary who was an astute observer and a prodigious note-taker. His diary has been described as "the most intimate record we have or ever can have of Abraham Lincoln in the White House." Nothing will bring you closer to Lincoln during this critical period.

McClellan, George B. *The Civil War Papers of George B. McClellan: Selected Correspondence, 1861-1865.* Ed. Stephen W. Sears. New York: Tichnor & Fields, 1989. A significant contribution by Sears that required hundreds of hours of searching and transcribing

McClellan's original papers in the Library of Congress.
"Reports." *The War of the Rebellion: A Compilation of the Official Records of the Union and Confederate Armies. Series 1, Vol. 19, Pt. 1.* Washington, D.C.: Government Printing Office, 1887. I've spent hundreds of hours of my life reading and re-reading the reports of officers, incessantly evaluating their observations, their agendas, and the "truths" they created.

"Reports, Correspondence, etc." *The War of the Rebellion: A Compilation of the Official Records of the Union and Confederate Armies. Series 1, Vol. 19, Pt. 2.* Washington, D.C.: Government Printing Office, 1887. My very favorite book of the campaign. It includes real-time correspondence and telegrams that place you in their saddles, at their field headquarters and at their command desks, immersing you right into their situations.

Welles, Gideon. *The Diary of Gideon Welles, Secretary of the Navy under Lincoln and Johnson.* New York: Houghton Mifflin Co., 1911. Another cabinet secretary who commented on much more than naval affairs and whose wit and wisdom brought Washington to life.

PARTICIPANT ACCOUNTS

There are multiple dozens of published participant accounts to choose from, but they are not exclusive to Antietam. Instead, they are published diaries, letters or journals written by soldiers who fought in the campaign and reference their experiences during those early weeks of September, 1862. The bibliographies of the books listed below will include extensive references to participant accounts. Be certain to discriminate between real-time accounts and reminiscences. Many of the most popular accounts are reflective reminiscences written twenty, thirty and forty years after the war and must be examined with suspicion.

I provide examples of questionable reminiscing in the text, some of which are from:

Johnson, Robert U. and Clarence C. Buel. ed. *Battles and Leaders of the Civil War,* Vol. II. New York: The Century Co., 1887.

CAMPAIGN STUDIES

Carmen, Ezra. *The Maryland Campaign of September, 1862: Vol. 1: South Mountain.* Ed. Thomas G. Clemens. New York: Savas Beatie, 2010. Dr. Clemens is one of my best friends. He spent a decade prior to the publication of this book "living daily" with Carmen —a Civil War veteran who fought at Antietam and who became the official government historian of the campaign. Following this publication, Tom spent nearly another decade working on the two volumes below.

Carmen, Ezra. *The Maryland Campaign of September, 1862: Vol. 2: Antietam.* Ed. Thomas G. Clemens. El Dorado Hills, CA: Savas Beatie, 2012. Carmen produced a voluminous campaign manuscript that never was published. The published trilogy cited here is an intentional division by subject matter.

Carmen, Ezra. *The Maryland Campaign of September, 1862: Vol. 3: Shepherdstown Ford and the End of the Campaign.* Ed. Thomas G. Clemens. El Dorado Hills, CA: Savas Beatie, 2017. Carmen's combined works are the most detailed and comprehensive examination of the campaign, based not only on reports and correspondence, but from a preponderance of post-war soldiers' reminiscences collected by Carmen in the late 19th and early 20th centuries.

Frye, Dennis E. *Antietam Revealed: The Battle of Antietam and the Maryland Campaign as You Have Never Seen it Before.* Collingswood, NJ: C. W. Historicals, LLC, 2004. A bullet-point reference guide that provides rapid access to people, actions and events during the campaign. Also examines the period after the battle, the government establishment of the battlefield and present-day preservation efforts.

Gallagher, Gary W., ed. *Antietam: Essays on the 1862 Maryland Campaign*. Kent: Kent State University Press, 1989. Introspective musings by the "quad-four" historians and co-founders of the modern-day battlefield preservation movement (Gallagher, Krick, Greene and Frye). Gary is editor of many volumes, but this is among his first.

Harsh, Joseph L. *Taken at the Flood: Robert E. Lee & Confederate Strategy in the Maryland Campaign of 1862*. Kent: Kent State University Press, 1999. I knew Dr. Harsh for 25 years and debated him for his pro-McClellan stances. His study of Lee during this period synthesizes decades of research and scholarly thought.

Hartwig, D. Scott. *To Antietam Creek: The Maryland Campaign of September, 1862*. Baltimore: The Johns Hopkins University Press, 2012. A monumental tome written by a fellow historian who spent his career working at Gettysburg. I was the first to present the final edition to Scott, whence I announced: "It's bigger than the Bible." And this volume is all preludes, ending on the day previous to the Battle of Antietam.

Jamieson, Perry D. *Death in September: The Antietam Campaign*. Fort Worth: Ryan Place Publishers, 1995. Dr. Jamieson spent his career as an Air Force historian, but his passion has always been the Civil War, and particularly Antietam—so much so that he selected Sharpsburg as his retirement location.

Luvaas, Jay and Harold W. Nelson, ed. *Guide to the Battle of Antietam: The Maryland Campaign of 1862*. Lawrence: The University Press of Kansas, 1987. Includes numerous primary documents, such as reports and correspondence, designed as a field guide to teach leadership to military commanders.

Murfin, James V. *The Gleam of Bayonets: The Battle of Antietam and the Maryland Campaign*. New York: A. S. Barnes & Co., 1964. The second most popular book on the campaign (based upon sales over the past 50 years). Published at the time of the Civil War centennial. My favorite study as I was growing up.

Palfrey, Francis Winthrop. *The Antietam and Fredericksburg.* New York: Charles Scribner's Sons, 1882. The first major popular study on the campaign, written by a Civil War veteran who fought in the West Woods at Antietam.

Rafus, Ethan S. *Antietam, South Mountain & Harpers Ferry: A Battlefield Guide.* Lincoln: University of Nebraska Press, 2008. The professor from the U. S. Army Command and General Staff College in Leavenworth guides each of us on a stop by stop staff ride at three different battlefields.

Reardon, Carol and Thomas Vosser. *A Field Guide to Antietam: Experiencing the Battlefield through its History, Places & People.* Always energetic and insightful, Dr. Reardon is one of the few academic scholars who also mastered the art of battlefield guiding.

Sears, Stephen W. *Landscape Turned Red: The Battle of Antietam.* New York: Ticknor & Fields, 1983. Sears's book has sold more copies than any other on this topic, outdistancing all competitors in sales by tens of thousands of books.

ANTIETAM

Alexander, Ted. *The Battle of Antietam: The Bloodiest Day.* Charleston, SC: The History Press, 2011. A concise one-day read published as part of the *Civil War Sesquicentennial Series* and written by one of my best friends who served as Antietam's historian for nearly three decades.

Ernst, Kathleen A. *Too Afraid to Cry: Maryland Civilians in the Antietam Campaign.* Mechanicsburg, PA: Stackpole Books, 1999. An outstanding study showing the effects of war upon the unwitting and unwilling. This book reveals the plight of the innocent farmers and villagers who hosted these bloody dramas.

McPherson, James M. *Crossroads of Freedom: Antietam: The Battle that Changed the Course of the Civil War*. New York: Oxford University Press, 2002. My friend Dr. McPherson (and Pulitzer Prize winner) is the first to tell you his is a study of the consequences of Antietam and not a book about the battle. The long-time Princeton professor particularly examines the relationship between Antietam and the Preliminary Emancipation Proclamation as well as upon diplomatic relations.

Priest, John Michael. *Antietam: The Soldiers' Battle*. Shippensburg, PA: White Mane Publishing Co., Inc., 1989. "Mr. Priest," as his history students at South Hagerstown High School called him, shared with me on Friday night visits into the Western Maryland Room of the Washington County Library dozens of original accounts he had discovered that previously were unpublished or lost in time.

Schildt, John W. *Four Days in October*. Privately printed, 1978 (and reprinted since). An excellent short study by one of Antietam's most prodigious explorers (and a friend for 50 years) on President Lincoln's visit to McClellan and his review of the army at Harpers Ferry and Antietam during the first week of October, 1862.

HARPERS FERRY

Frye, Dennis E. *Harpers Ferry Under Fire: A Border Town during the American Civil War*. Virginia Beach: The Donning Co. Publishers, 2012. The U.S. Armory and Arsenal town made famous by John Brown was nearly destroyed during the war. Situated on the border between North and South, the town changed hands eight times and hosted five battles.

Frye, Dennis E. *History and Tour Guide of Stonewall Jackson's Battle of Harpers Ferry*. A detailed examination of the biggest battle fought in present-day West Virginia that resulted in the largest surrender of U.S. soldiers during the Civil War.

SOUTH MOUNTAIN

Hoptak, John David. *The Battle of South Mountain*. Charleston, SC: The History Press, 2011. A fast moving and easily understandable written by an excellent National Park Service interpreter and historian and published as part of the Civil War Sesquicentennial Series.

Priest, John Michael. *Before Antietam: The Battle for South Mountain*. Shippensburg, PA: White Mane Publishing Co. Inc., 1992. A detailed examination of the fighting at each of the gaps in an unfolding drama revealing Lee's attempt to block McClellan's legions.

Reese, Timothy J. *Sealed with their Lives: The Battle for Crampton's Gap, Burkittsville, MD, September 14, 1862*. Butternut & Blue, 1998. A thorough analysis of the action at the southern-most gap in the Battle for South Mountain and the Union army's failure to fully exploit its advantages.

ROBERT E. LEE

Freeman, Douglas Southall. *R. E. Lee: A Biography*. Vol. II. New York: Charles Scribner's Sons, 1934. Nothing comparable to the exhaustive four-volume study of Lee by the Pulitzer Prize winner from Richmond. The second volume contains chapters on the first invasion and Antietam, including Freeman's curious defense of Lee's performance.

Freeman, Douglas Southall. *Lee's Lieutenants: A Study in Command: Cedar Mountain to Chancellorsville*. Vol. II. New York: Charles Scribner's Sons, 1943. Freeman's meticulous research inserts you into the command circle of Jackson, Longstreet, Stuart and other top Lee surrogates.

GEORGE B. MCCLELLAN

Hassler, Warren W. Jr. *General George B. McClellan: Shield of the Union*. Baton Rouge: Louisiana State University Press, 1957. As the title suggests, an unabashed defense of McClellan and a dangerous profession.

McClellan, George B. *McClellan's Own Story*. New York: Webster, 1887. The general's self-defense written during a time when no one was defending him. Don't let the original publication date deter you; the book has been reprinted multiple times, proving a continuing fascination with Little Mac.

Rafuse, Ethan S. *McClellan's War: The Failure of Moderation in the Struggle for the Union*. Bloomington: Indiana University Press, 2011. The most recent biography on McClellan by a professor at the Fort Leavenworth Army Command and General Staff College.

Sears, Stephen W. *George B. McClellan: The Young Napoleon*. New York: Ticknor & Fields, 1983. The most widely published book on McClellan in history, and the antithesis of the Hassler study.

ANTIETAM PHOTOGRAPHY

Frassanito, William A. *Antietam: The Photographic Legacy of America's Bloodiest Day*. New York: Charles Scribner's Sons, 1978. Groundbreaking "then-and-now" study that discovered the original locations on the battlefield of dozens of the post-battle photographs.

Zeller, Bob and John J. Richter and Garry E. Adelman. *Antietam in 3-D. Center for Civil War Photography*, 2012. A fascinating publication that includes some of the best examples of the 1862 stereoscopic photographs shot on the battlefield. 3-D glasses included!

Acknowledgements

We often speak of heroes, but seldom do we mention teachers in the same sentence with our police officers, fire fighters and veterans. We should . . . always.

Heroes are people we admire and respect for dedicating their lives to helping others, protecting people and defending our human rights. Teachers excel at this. They give unselfishly, year after year; and their return on investment is not a Wall Street pension, but each of their students who becomes a productive and contributing citizen that benefits us all.

Unfortunately, we give teachers little credit for their selfless commitment of their time and devotion to each of us. We take them for granted, pay most of them miserable wages, and give them grief for never doing enough. But who would any of us be, and where would we be, without our teachers?

I was reminded of their immense value while in the Capitol building at Charleston, West Virginia during the "55 strong" teacher strike in March, 2018. I was there because the West Virginia Senate was honoring me with a resolution for my career as Chief Historian at Harpers Ferry National Historical Park. That moment I'll never forget. But even more memorable were the thousands of teachers packed into the Capitol and hundreds seated in the Senate gallery, epitomizing our First Amendment rights. As Senator John Unger presented the resolution, he focused on my own 40-year role as an educator and the teachers gave me a standing ovation. I walked into the chamber clapping for them, for they truly deserved the ovation.

So for anyone who reads this volume, please pause for a moment—and reflect upon your teachers. You couldn't read this without them; and you certainly couldn't comprehend the provocation herein without them teaching you how to be good thinkers. Remember your teachers for who they really are—heroes.

As a professional historian, I thank my mentors and colleagues who have helped me "think" about history for the past forty years. Those of particular note include Ted Alexander, Edwin C. Bearss, Dr. James Broomall, Dr. Millard Bushong, Dr. Pete Carmichael, Dr. Thomas Clemens, William "Jack" Davis, Dr. Kitty Frescoln, Dr. Gary Gallagher, Richard Gillespie, A. Wilson Greene, Dr. Allen Guelzo, Dr. Joseph Harsh, John Hennessy, Dr. James Holland, John King, Robert K. Krick, Dr. Richard McMurry, Dr. James McPherson, Michael Musick, James Ogden, Dr. Stephen Potter, Dr. Carol Reardon, Dr. James I. "Bud" Robertson, Dr. Richard Sommers, Dr. Mark Snell, Dr. John Stealey, Dr. Jerry Thomas and Dr. Jill Titus. To each of you, I am grateful for your encouragement, scholarship, and most important, your friendship.

Perhaps my best teachers of all have been my parents, John and Janice Poffenberger Frye. Not only did they teach me history, they ensured I learned and respected the history that surrounded me as I grew up as a kid so near Antietam, South Mountain and Harpers Ferry. They've spent the past six decades promoting and preserving history, with Dad in the lead and Mom always in support. What role models you both have been.

A special thank you to the dozens upon dozens of Civil War organizations, as well as colleges and universities, who have invited me to lecture before their audiences or lead tours for them on the battlefields. Every concept in this book has been presented before live audiences, and the feedback and response has helped fashion *Antietam Shadows'* contents.

I can write a book, but I cannot produce one. I am blessed to have the remarkable talents and skills of Beth and Tim Rowland as designers and editors. They metamorphose my drafts into art. I so appreciate the hours they devote to the plethora of details necessary to produce this volume. To my dear friend Susan Haberkorn, who once worked as a professional copy editor, thank you for employing your careful eyes to every word, letter and punctuation mark. Tough business. To Ryan Harpster, thank you for taking complex maps (found in most Civil War books) and simplifying them for appeal to a much larger audience. I asked Ryan to emphasize geography rather than tactics, as many people who read this are not familiar with the region.

I reserve my final and most important acknowledgement for my wife Sylvia and my dogs, "Mr. Lincoln" and "Bonnie Blue"—because they are with me always, and supporting me every day—and that means more than anything else.

—

Index

and McLaws, 63, 106-108
Miles's defense during, 62-65,
69-71, 102-104
Miles delays Jackson, 69-71,
102-103
and mountain elevations, 70-
71
and South Mountain, 98, 103
and surrender, 104, 117, 226-
227
Harpers Ferry Military Commission
and "cows' tails order," 204
appointed to investigate Harpers Ferry disaster, 201
and Halleck's testimony
against McClellan, 202-203
investigations of, 201-202
censures McClellan, 202-204
condemns Miles, 201-202
politics of, 201-204
Harpers Ferry Road
and John Brown, 165
and most direct route for Confederates to Antietam, 164-
166.
map showing, 145
Harrisburg, Pennsylvania
and possible Confederate
target, 45
Harsh, Dr. Joseph
defends McClellan, 31-32
Hawthorne, Nathaniel
on power of words, 11
musing on duplicity, 109
Higginson, Thomas Wentworth
musing on originality, 77
Hill, Daniel Harvey
and Bloody Lane, 150-151, 232
and Lost Order, 29-30, 215

History
and absolutes, 17, 20
and author's destiny, 1
on challenging convention, 5,
10, 144
and character traits, 10
as chronology, 4, 7, 9, 20, 41-42
condition of, 7
creation of, 2-3, 8-9
as dates, 17, 20
as debate, 3, 9
dependent upon, 9
as drama, 41-42
as disagreement, 11-12
Emerson's musings about, 2
as emotion, 95
as exaggeration, 4-5, 89, 149
as fable, 1
as facts, 2, 8-9, 30
as judgment, 3-4
and leadership, 10
as lies, 162
as memory, 4-5
as mentor, 9-10
as mystery, 30
Napoleon's definition of, 1
as opinion, 2
as options, 42
as perception, 2-3
as point of view, 3, 98
as prejudice, 2-3
as primary source, 149
as provocation, 10
as recollections, 4-5, 150-154
as replay, 41-42
rejection of, 7-8, 20
repeats itself, 9
teaching of, 4, 7-9, 20, 42, 51
as truth, 2
as simplistic, 4

Made in the USA
Middletown, DE
22 November 2022

15802111R00159